MATH
AND
LITERATURE
(K–3)
Book Two

MATH AND LITERATURE

(K–3)

Book Two

by Stephanie Sheffield
Introduction by Marilyn Burns

MATH SOLUTIONS PUBLICATIONS

Editorial direction by Lorri Ungaretti
Design and production by Aileen Friedman

Copyright ©1995 by Math Solutions Publications

Printed in the United States of America.

ISBN 0-941355-11-X

Distributed by Cuisenaire Company of America, Inc.
P.O. Box 5026
White Plains, NY 10602-5026
(800) 237-3142

Marilyn Burns Education Associates is dedicated to improving mathematics education. For information about Math Solutions courses, resource materials, and services, write or call:

Marilyn Burns Education Associates
150 Gate 5 Road, Suite 101
Sausalito, CA 94965
Telephone (415) 332-4181
Fax (415) 331-1931

ACKNOWLEDGMENTS

Special thanks to the teachers who allowed me to teach lessons in their classrooms.

Teachers in Beneke Elementary School, Spring Independent School District, Houston, Texas

Marcia Bancroft

Mary Karnick

Sarah Mallow

Doris Pauley

Sandra Yates

Teachers in Brill Elementary School, Klein Independent School District, Houston, Texas

Connie Cooper

Wisha Rose

Special thanks to those teachers who contributed their insights and expertise by sharing their classroom experiences with me.

Rusty Bresser, Laurel Elementary School, Oceanside, California

Marilyn Burns, Park School, Mill Valley, California

Min Hong, P.S. 11, New York, New York

Dee Uyeda, Park School, Mill Valley, California

Thanks also to those people who helped me make this book a reality.

To my children, Megan and Patrick, who fill my life with joy and share with me a love of literature.

To my husband, Carl, for his patience while I used more than my share of the family computer time. His quiet support allowed me to do this work.

To my mother, Ann Mueller, who filled our home with books.

To Dorothy Jenett, who taught me to love learning and believe in myself.

To Marilyn Burns, whose friendship and encouragement have helped me see mathematics and myself in a new way. The insights she shares and the questions she asks continue to challenge and change me.

To Katharine Kharas, for teaching me mathematics and loving me.

To Math Solutions consultants, whose love for children and dedication to mathematics education inspire me daily.

CONTENTS

INTRODUCTION

I'm delighted to introduce *Math and Literature (K-3), Book Two,* by Stephanie Sheffield. In this book, Stephanie presents mathematics lessons based on 21 children's books. For each book Stephanie describes what actually happened when she taught the lesson and includes student work to show how the children responded and the mathematics they did.

Stephanie is well qualified to write this book. She loves children's books and spends a good deal of her spare time combing the children's departments of bookstores. (Having seven-year-old twins helps her to justify this passion.) She has thought deeply about helping students make sense of mathematics and is an instructor of Math Solutions inservice courses. In addition, Stephanie is an experienced elementary teacher, currently teaching first grade in Spring Independent School District in Houston, Texas.

The book evolved from my book *Math and Literature (K-3),* which was published in 1992. After I wrote the book, I kept finding more children's books that were useful for helping children learn to think and reason mathematically. I tried new lessons, talked with other teachers, and shared ideas with friends.

During this period, Stephanie communicated with me from time to time about the ways she was using children's books in math lessons. After I received a half dozen or so notes from her describing lessons she had done with her class, I suggested that we collaborate on a sequel to *Math and Literature (K-3).* My plan was that we would continue teaching lessons, send them to each other, try out each other's ideas, and compile a collection to fill a book.

However, as Stephanie continued to send me ideas, I found myself more interested in trying her suggestions than in creating new ones of my own. Her lessons were wonderful. They exposed children to mathematical ideas in fresh and engaging ways. The students I taught loved them. And I found Stephanie's write-ups enjoyable to read, clear, and inspiring. I suggested that she take ownership of the book and make it fully her own, and she agreed. Stephanie worked on the book with enthusiasm and energy. She wrote about her experiences, collected student work, and did all the revising a book demands. Also, she communicated with other teachers and incorporated some of their experiences as well.

Math and Literature (K–3), Book Two is similar in several ways to the book that I wrote. First, the teaching ideas are firmly based in the notion that children learn best when they are actively involved. Stephanie's lessons are full of suggestions for engaging children fully. Second, the book honors the importance of children's mathematical experience extending beyond arithmetic skills. The lessons involve students with ideas that include shape recognition, symmetry, graphing, logical reasoning, measuring, estimating, and using money. They also help children become flexible in thinking about numbers and developing their number sense. And third, the book recognizes that the mathematics is an educational bonus that can emerge from the children's books, but that reading and enjoying books is valuable education in itself.

Stephanie's book differs from *Math and Literature (K–3)* in several aspects. The first book had sample lessons for 10 books and brief write-ups of ideas for 20 additional books. Stephanie's book focuses on a total of 21 books (and one poem) but presents fully developed sample lessons for each, resulting in a longer resource that is rich in detail. In a way, Stephanie's work represents the growth we've made in thinking more deeply about the ways to incorporate children's books into math instruction. Also, Stephanie includes ideas for using some of the books at several grade levels, thus broadening the usefulness of the books for classroom instruction.

In the 11 years that I've known Stephanie, I've come to admire and respect her deep commitment to teaching, her keen intelligence, and the clarity of her thinking. It was a joy working with her on this book, and I'm proud to publish it. I'm convinced that you and your students will benefit from Stephanie's experience and wisdom.

Marilyn Burns
1994

The Bedspread

> *The Bedspread,* by Sylvia Fair, is the story of two elderly sisters who live at opposite ends of a very long bed. Maud and Amelia live a boring life and even have a boring white bedspread. One day they hit upon the idea of embroidering the bedspread with memories of the house they lived in during their long-ago childhood. Each sister stitches on her own side of the bedspread. The two women try to embroider the same things but are surprised when they see their different handiwork. The book leads to an activity that gives children experience with Venn diagrams and symmetry.

"**I** have a book to share that has an important mathematical idea in it," I told the class of second graders. "But, most of all, I think it's a good story."

The children settled down on the floor and listened intently. They were intrigued by the idea of sisters who live in a bed. The class giggled when the sisters got into a "No, it's not"/"Yes, it is" argument.

After I read the pages that describe Maud and Amelia stitching the doors of their houses, I stopped reading for a minute. "Their doors are alike in some ways and different in others. Who can tell me one way the doors are different?" I held the book so that the class could see the pictures. Audrey raised her hand.

"Maud's door is purple and Amelia's is blue," she said. I went to the board and drew two large, interlocking circles for a Venn diagram. I wrote *Maud* over the left circle and *Amelia* over the right circle. In Maud's circle I wrote *purple,* and in Amelia's circle I wrote *blue.*

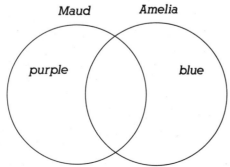

"Who can tell me another way the doors are different?" I asked.

"Maud's door is neat and Amelia's door is messy," Kendra said. I wrote *neat* in Maud's circle and *messy* in Amelia's circle.

After collecting several more differences, I asked, "How are the doors the same?"

Joanne responded, "They both have a door knocker."

"Yes, they do," I said. "The door knockers don't look alike, but there's one on each door. Where do you think that should go up here?" I pointed to the Venn diagram on the board.

"In the middle," Antonio said. I pointed to the intersection of the two circles and looked at Antonio. He nodded, and I wrote *door knocker* in the space. Antonio's idea was mathematically correct, but others seemed confused by it. I tried to explain. I placed my finger in the intersection and said, "By writing it here, I'm putting it in both Maud's circle and Amelia's circle." I traced each circle with my finger as I mentioned it.

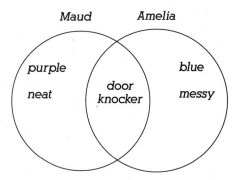

Then I traced the circle with Maud's name over it. "What can you tell me about the things in this circle?" I asked.

"Those are things on Maud's door," Janine answered.

Next I traced the circle with Amelia's name over it. Scott said, "Those are things about Amelia's door."

"What about here in the middle?" I asked.

"Those are things in both their houses," Jane explained.

"This is a Venn diagram," I said. "It's a way to organize information when we want to tell how things are alike and different. You'll have a chance to make a Venn diagram of your own a little later."

I continued reading the book. The children were interested in every picture and commented on the illustrations. This surprised me a little, because the illustrations do not have bold colors or exciting action; they depict embroidery stitches in subdued colors.

This is a book that children might overlook on the library shelf, but my students loved it. They were drawn in by the story and looked carefully to see how the sisters interpreted each idea. The students told me later that they thought the pictures matched the story perfectly. After reading the book and having the children talk about their favorite parts, I posed a question.

"Who can explain what the word 'symmetry' means?" I asked.

Antonio answered, "It's when you have something where one half is just like the other half." I generally find Antonio's math understanding impressive.

"Does anyone else have an idea about symmetry?" I asked.

Debbie raised her hand. "If something has symmetry and you put a mirror down the middle, it looks the same."

"The same as what?" I then asked.

"The same as the other side," she said.

"Was the bedspread symmetrical?" I asked.

"Sort of," Alex said. "They both have a house, a chimney, and a garden. But they're really not the same."

"They don't look the same. Maybe the sisters should've told each other what they were doing," Janine suggested.

"But then it wouldn't be so pretty," said Joanne.

I then introduced the activity to the class. I arranged the class in pairs and had them sit so partners were across from each other at a desk. I distributed one sheet of 12-by-18-inch white construction paper to each pair and called for the children's attention.

"You and your partner will create houses, just as Maud and Amelia did," I explained, "but you'll draw yours instead of sew them. Since the sisters couldn't see each other's work until the end, I'm giving you two folders to stand up between the two of you, so you can't see your partner's work." I held up two folders, the kind with pockets on both sides. I demonstrated how to open the folders and stand them so they divided the paper in half.

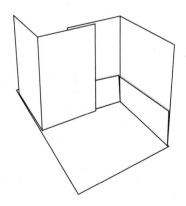

"If you can't see your partner's work, how will you know if you're drawing the same things?" I asked.

"Can we talk to each other?" Kendra asked.

"Absolutely," I responded. "You'll need to take turns drawing a part of the picture and describing it to each other with as much detail as possible. You might want to give your partner information about the position of what you're drawing. You may also want to talk about its shape and color. The more information you give your partner, the more symmetry will be in your final picture." The children set up their desks with the papers and folders and began to work.

Right away, Hassan and Jed raised their hands. "Can we draw a castle instead of a house?" Hassan asked.

"Sure," I said, and the boys got to work. When I walked by a few minutes later, Jed was explaining his drawing in detail. "Now put a tower on the left of the door and one on the edge of the castle, and connect them with a bridge. Make sure you make small bricks and make the roof pointed like a triangle." I watched as Hassan listened and reacted to Jed's directions. "Uh huh," he said, and "okay," and "yeah." But when I looked at Hassan's paper, I realized how different Hassan's version was.

Although Jed and Hassan talked in great detail as they worked, their two castles looked quite different.

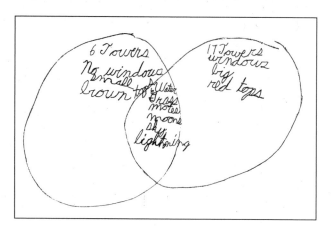

When the boys finished their drawings, they eagerly lifted the folders and looked at each other's work. "Wow! You put the tower there!" Jed exclaimed. They turned the paper around and looked carefully at each other's pictures, pointing out the differences they noticed. They called me over to look with them.

"I think your castles are both great," I said. "Now I want you to make your own Venn diagram to explain the similarities and differences you've noticed. You can write your names above the circles the way we did for Maud's and Amelia's doors."

Janine and Thalia brought me their pictures. I asked, "How did you help each other understand where you were drawing things on your picture?"

Janine said, "I told Thalia to draw windows with four little windows in them, but she made hers square and I made mine round at the top. I didn't tell her what shape to make them." As I had done with Hassan and Jed, I asked the two girls to make a Venn diagram for their pictures.

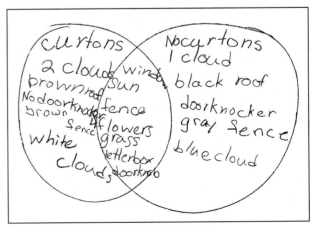

Thalia and Janine drew two very similar houses but were able to find seven differences.

All of the children were excited to lift the folders and compare their houses, and they were eager for me to look at their pictures. After talking with each pair of students about how they had communicated, I directed them to make a Venn diagram to show how their finished houses were alike and different.

The next day I asked pairs of children to share their pictures with the class and talk about their experiences. Students talked about how difficult it was to give clear directions to their partners.

"You had to tell them what to draw and where to put it," Audrey observed.

"And what the shape was," Kendra added.

I think this lesson provided an opportunity for children to think about symmetry and use geometric language in a new way.

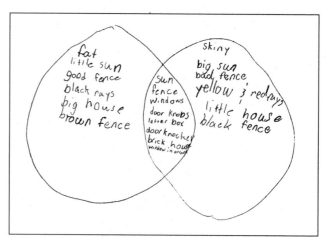

Kendra and Alex listed eight items their houses had in common and six items that had different attributes.

Benny's Pennies

In *Benny's Pennies*, written by Pat Brisson, Benny McBride has five new pennies and wants to spend them on his family and his pets. He finds something special to buy for each—a rose for his mother, a cookie for his brother, a paper hat for his sister, a meaty bone for his dog, and a floppy fish for his cat. This story provides an engaging way to introduce kindergartners and first graders to ways of counting and handling money.

I read *Benny's Pennies* to my first graders after we had worked informally with money for a few months. They were eager to predict what would happen on each page. When Benny bought the rose, Nina spoke up, "It's for his mother!" Eddie commented, "Now he has four pennies."

As I read each page, the class discussed who the gift was for and how much money Benny had left. I allowed them to talk to one another as I read, and their discussion was animated and to the point. Although the book was simple, they enjoyed hearing it and retelling it.

We acted out the story a few times, and then I could see that the children were ready for a new challenge. "Let's write our own version of the story," I suggested.

"We could call it *Jenny's Pennies,*" Sharon said.

"Okay," I responded. "What do we need to put into our story?"

The children decided we needed a main character (Jenny), some friends to give her advice about what to buy, a list of things to buy, and some money. We spent some time talking about and recording words of advice from Jenny's friends, and chose our five favorite things on the list to include in the book:

> something bright and delicious (Skittles candy)
> something pretty that you can play with (a doll)
> something plastic that holds water (a cup)
> something colorful for writing (markers)
> something with laces for running (sneakers)

Next I asked the children how much they thought Jenny should pay for each item. "The Skittles should cost a penny, like the things in the book," Timothy said.

"Then the doll should be twice as much," Eddie suggested. This puzzled some children who weren't familiar with the phrase "twice as much."

"Can you explain for us what 'twice as much' means, Eddie?" I asked.

"I mean like double," he said. "Two is twice as much as one, so the doll should cost two cents. It's like when you roll doubles on dice." I watched the faces of the other students to see who registered a look of understanding and who seemed still to be unsure.

"How about another example?" I asked. "How much is twice as much as three? Tell the person next to you what you think."

After Cassie tried to explain to Mary why she thought it was six, she raised her hand and asked if she could use pennies from our class penny jar. I gave her a handful and she put out a row of three and another row of three under it. "There," she said, "I doubled it. Now you try, Mary." Cassie made a row of five pennies and Mary placed five pennies under it.

"5 and 5 is 10. Now I get it!" Mary said. Other students who noticed how Cassie had used the pennies came to the front of the room to get their own pennies from the penny jar.

After a few minutes of exploring the idea of twice as much, I refocused the students' attention on our story. "Who can tell how much the cup should cost if we use Eddie's pattern of doubling?"

Maya raised her hand. "2 and 2 is 4," she said. "That's double, so the cup is four cents," she said. I recorded *4 cents* on the board next to the description of the cup. I also recorded the prices of the Skittles and the doll. Kimberly suggested eight cents for the markers, the next item on our list, and I saw heads around the room nod in agreement.

The final price proved more difficult. "But you can't get 8 on one dice, " Harlan said. He had used the dots on dice to add the other numbers. Next to him, Nina moved eight pennies into a row, and used Harlan's pennies to make another row.

"It's 16!" he exclaimed.

Around the room, students pooled their pennies to verify the answer. When they were all satisfied, we moved on.

(Note: I decided to continue with Eddie's doubling suggestion and use it as the basis for the rest of the lesson. The plan I had in mind before Eddie suggested doubling was to ask the children to think of some sort of pattern we might use for the prices of the items for our story. I had thought that perhaps a child would suggest that the amounts go by 5s, with the first costing 5 cents, the second 10 cents, and so on. Or a child might suggest that each item cost two cents more than the one before instead of one cent more. Then students could figure out how much money was needed altogether. I think that when I do this lesson again, I'll try my original plan. If no student suggests a pattern, then I'll suggest one.)

"I've noticed something different about our story from the book we read," I said. "In *Benny's Pennies*, we knew from the beginning that Benny had five pennies, but in our story we don't know how many pennies Jenny will need to make all of her purchases. Do you think you could figure that out?"

Most of the students seemed confident about their ability to do this. I told them they could find a partner with whom to work or choose to work alone, and I distributed paper for their solutions. "Remember to explain with words, numbers, or pictures how you figure out the answer," I reminded them.

Many students used pennies to solve the problem. Some drew circles to represent the pennies. I noticed that while most of the children were counting the pennies by 1s, Alex and Conner were making groups of 10s and 1s. Having children work on a problem like this allows me to observe their approaches and informally assess their understanding.

When I called the class back together, I asked students to present their solutions. Ronnie and Timothy went first. They came up to the front of the room and showed their paper. Ronnie read, "We drew the pennies and counted by 2s. We had one left over and that made 31 cents."

Audrey and Harlan stood next to their desks for their presentation and pointed to the groups of 1, 2, 4, 8, and 16 pennies they had arranged. "We got 31 too. We counted by 1s," Audrey reported.

Alex and Conner had also made groups of 1, 2, 4, 8, and 16. They explained how they took the 2 pennies and put them with the 8 pennies to make 10 pennies. They made two more groups of 10, using the pennies from the group of 4 and the group of 16. One penny was left over.

Having children explain how they reason provides the kind of informal peer teaching that is valuable for helping children think about counting objects in different ways. We agreed that Jenny needed 31 cents. It was the end of class, and I promised we'd continue work on our book the next day.

For the next day, I prepared a plastic sandwich bag for each table with one quarter, four dimes, six nickels, and 35 pennies in it. I think it's important for children to use real money to solve problems. Plastic money doesn't look, sound, or feel like real coins, and as adults we use all of those attributes to identify money. We can all tell when we reach into our pockets which coins we have, just by how they feel. We're familiar with the sound coins make when they jingle together and can probably identify some by their sound. Children need opportunities to handle real money in order to develop that same familiarity.

I asked the class to think about different assortments of coins Jenny could use to have 31 cents to pay for all the things she bought. I then showed the children how they were to record their ideas. I gave each pair of students a sheet of paper and demon-strated.

"Fold it in half, then in half again the other way," I explained as I demonstrated. "How many boxes do you think your paper will have when you open it?" Some children predicted, and others folded and opened the paper to count.

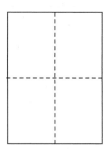

"Your problem is to think of four different ways Jenny might have a total of 31 cents to pay for her purchases," I said. "When you both agree that you have one way to make 31 cents, come to the table in the front. On the table are coin stamps and stamp pads. Record your answer in one box on your paper by stamping to show which coins you used. Then go back to your seat and find another way to make 31 cents."

The children were eager and interested in this problem. It was related to the *Jenny's Pennies* book they were making, and using real money and coin stamps was highly motivating. The stamps I had available showed both the fronts and backs of coins. Although the children were not as familiar with the stamps of the backs, they had the actual coins with them as they recorded their answers, so they just turned the coins over to make the match.

The students used coin stamps to record their answers.

Kimberly and Sharon were the first to fill up their four squares. They brought their paper to me, and I had them take turns counting the money they had stamped. This gave me the chance to assess informally what they had done and to see if they both understood their solutions. I watched to see how they counted the coins. Did they begin with the largest denomination or did they start randomly? Did they make the transition smoothly from counting by 10s to counting by 5s or did they hesitate? Did they point to each coin as they counted it or did they have another way to keep track of which ones they had already counted? When the girls finished counting, I asked if they could think of any other ways to make 31 cents with coins.

"Are there more?" Kimberly asked. "We filled up all the squares!"

"I know of at least one more way it can be done with the coins in your baggie," I told them. "If you find another way, turn your paper over and record it in one of the boxes on the back." They ran back to their seats to look for another solution.

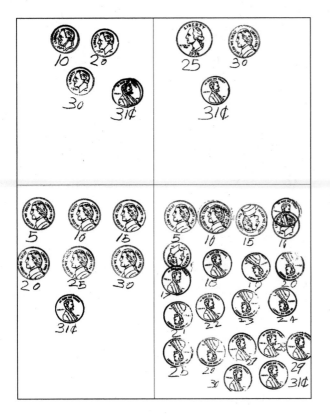

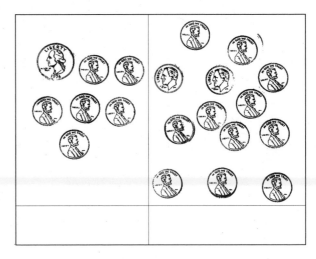

When Kimberly and Sharon learned that there were more than four solutions to the problem, they turned over their paper and found two more ways to get 31 cents.

After each pair had found at least four solutions, I called the class together. "Let's share what we've found," I said. I let each pair of children choose one solution to share aloud. I asked them to tell us how many of each coin they used to make 31 cents. I encouraged the others to listen carefully to see if they could identify the solution presented as the same as one of their own. If they did, they were to put a check in that box and to try to find a different solution to share.

The first graders had difficulty comparing their solutions with the ones being described. If their own coins were placed in the box differently from the way someone else called them out, it was hard for them to identify the coins and keep track. But I think it was good listening practice for them anyway. There are many things I think we should ask children to do without expecting proficiency.

The class was amazed at how many different solutions there were. As children presented, I recorded their solutions on the board as a way to keep track of them. After three pairs had reported, the chart looked like this:

Quarters	Dimes	Nickels	Pennies
0	3	0	1
1	0	1	1
0	1	4	1

"Hey, there's a pattern!" Timothy exclaimed. "There's always one in the pennies column."

"That's because it's always thirty-ONE cents," Conner told him. I could see that what seemed obvious to Conner was a curious pattern to Timothy.

"I did it with six pennies," Kimberly said, showing how she and Sharon had stamped one quarter and six pennies. Both Conner and Timothy looked surprised.

When we left the problem, I had recorded eight different ways on the chart. Some students were still not convinced that we had found all the possible ways to make 31 cents. (We hadn't; there are 18 ways in all.) I left the bags of coins and the coin stamps in the math center for students to continue to explore. We finished our work with *Benny's Pennies* by writing and illustrating our class book and sharing it with another class.

Nina had difficulty recording the correct number as she counted the coins.

Sharing the Book with a Kindergarten Class

When I read this book to kindergartners, they'd already had some experience identifying coins. I showed the picture of Benny as he started out in the morning. Covering up the part of the picture that showed his hand holding one penny, I said, "How many pennies does he have in this hand?"

"Four," answered Ruben.

"So how many pennies do you think are in his other hand?" I asked. "One!" some students called out.

I stopped after I read the page where Benny asked for advice about what to buy.

"He should buy a candy cane," Julio suggested.

"Yeah, a candy cane," others agreed.

"What else could he buy?" I asked.

"A lollipop," suggested Jennifer.

"Some bubble gum," offered Vanessa.

"Let's see what he does buy," I said. I continued reading.

After Benny made his first purchase, Vanessa spoke up again. "Now he's only got four pennies," she said. She showed me four fingers. "But he's got one good thing, so it's still five."

After Benny bought the second item—the cookie—several children held up their hands to show me three fingers. They continued to show me their fingers as they counted down with the story.

When I read the book a second time, I asked the children to keep track of the numbers of pennies. At the beginning of the book, I asked how many pennies Benny had. They showed me five fingers.

"Show me on your other hand how many good things he has," I said. They held up their other hands with no fingers showing.

With each page I read, the children put down one finger on one hand and put up a finger on the other hand. With four fingers on one hand and one on the other, Kareem said, "It's still five showing."

"What do you mean, Kareem?" I asked.

"4 and 1 is 5!" Kareem was confident about all the combinations of 5.

Shontay, like some others, watched her friends before deciding if she had the correct number of fingers showing. Arturo and Yesinia just sat and enjoyed the book, without participating in the counting at all. This was fine with me. Children bring different things to mathematical experiences. Reading a book like *Benny's Pennies* can help some children reinforce their understanding, while leading others to expand their awareness of numbers.

A Cloak for the Dreamer

> *A Cloak for the Dreamer*, by Aileen Friedman, is the story of a tailor
> who has three sons. His older sons, Ivan and Alex, hope to become
> tailors; but Misha, the youngest, dreams of traveling far and wide.
> When the Archduke orders new cloaks, the tailor asks his sons for
> help. Ivan sews a cloak out of rectangular pieces of cloth. Alex uses
> squares and triangles. Misha fashions his cloak out of circles, and its
> open spaces make it useless. The tailor finds a (geometric) way to fix
> the cloak and allows Misha to fulfill his dream of going out into the
> world. The story presents students with a context for thinking about
> geometric shapes and how they fit together.

Rusty Bresser read *A Cloak for the Dreamer* to his third graders
near the end of the year. During the year, Rusty had provided
opportunities for his students to investigate quilting patterns and tessellations. He wondered how these earlier experiences might affect
the way his students thought about solving the problem of the holes
in Misha's cloak.

Before Rusty started to read the book, he showed the cover to his
class. Because the story is about a tailor and his three sons, Rusty
asked, "Who can explain what a tailor is?"

Artrina said, "Someone who sews clothes." Others nodded.

Rusty read the story up to the page where Misha has made his
cloak of circles. When Rusty showed the class the picture, he asked,
"What do you think about Misha's cloak?"

Scott said, "The cloak has holes in it. The Archduke will get water
on him."

"He'll get muddy," added Amber.

"It won't work, it's not solid," said Mark.

"I agree that Misha has a problem," Rusty responded. "What do
you think he should do about his problem? Who has an idea?"

Makito raised his hand. "I think if he put a blanket on the back of
it, it would cover up the holes," he said

Anna had another idea. She said, "If Misha made more circles, he
could sew them on the back where the holes are."

Josh suggested, "He could just make another cloak with rectangles instead of circles."

Mark offered a different solution. "He needs to cut the sides off the circles so they're hexagons," he said. "Then he can sew them together again."

Mark suggested that Misha fix the cloak by cutting the sides of the circles to make hexagons.

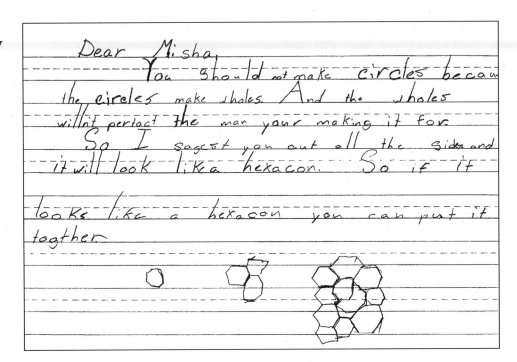

Dear Misha,

You should not make circles becau the circles make wholes. And the wholes willn't perfect the man your making it for. So I sagest you cut all the sides and it will look like a hexacon. So if it looks like a hexacon you can put it togther

Rusty reported that he thought it was important to give his students the opportunity to verbalize their ideas before asking them to write. "I wanted to have many ideas available," he said. "I think talking about various solutions provides some students with access to an idea that they might not have on their own. It also gives those children who have ideas a chance to formulate them verbally. Verbalization is a helpful support to the writing process."

Rather than continuing to read the story, Rusty asked the children to write letters to Misha offering him a solution to the problem. "When you write to Misha," he told the children, "first explain the problem with the cloak. Then offer Misha a solution and include an illustration to show him what you mean." Rusty asked for questions, and then the class got to work.

As they worked, the children talked to one another, sharing their solutions, talking about the book, and discussing their pictures. Rusty circulated and, as students finished, he had them read their letters aloud to him.

Jo Ann wrote: *Dear Misha, I have another answer if you lamanate it it could probaly be a rain cloak of the world. from your friind, Jo Ann.*

Sam wrote: *Dear Misha, The problem is you made a holes in the cloak. You should over lap where the holes were.*

"How would that solve his problem?" Rusty asked.

Sam thought for a moment and then decided to write some more about his solution. He added: *You wouldn't want the Archduke to get wet or get mad. And cut the sides.* He drew pictures to show his solution in three steps.

Sam suggested that Misha overlap the circles.

The next day Rusty called the students together on the rug to share their letters. They were interested in all the different solutions and laughed at the ones they thought were funny.

After the children had shared their work, Rusty read the book all the way through, starting over again from the beginning. Mark was excited to see that the tailor solved Misha's problem the same way he had suggested. Rusty let him enjoy this happy discovery but was careful to talk to the class about this not being the only possible answer.

Alicia wrote that Misha should use plastic and add a strap and a button.

Dear Misha,

Your cloak has holes in it. What were you thinking! lisen here bud all you have to do is put plstic that will fit it and then pu a strap and a butin that's all you have to bo o.K.

plastic's all ready on it. ⟶

I sugestied plastic because it would not spole the colors and it would not get on it

Rusty also asked the children how they felt about stopping in the middle of the book to solve a problem. This is something Rusty does not normally do because he feels it interrupts the flow of the story. The students decided that stopping in the middle was a good idea in this instance.

"It made us curious," said Annette.

"It gave us a reason to listen," Josh added.

Then Rusty presented a second activity. He handed out sheets of 12-by-18-inch white drawing paper and gave each group tagboard with two sizes of triangles, rectangles, and squares printed on it. (See blackline master on page 25.) He also put out stacks of colored construction paper.

"Each of you will choose one shape and cut it out of the tag board," Rusty explained. "Then you'll use the tagboard shape as a pattern to trace and cut more pieces from two different colors of construction paper. Use those shapes to make a pattern of your own for a cloak."

The children enjoyed the activity. They chose their colors carefully, thinking about how they would look together. When they finished making their cloak patterns, they taped them to the wall. The students stood together in small groups talking about the patterns they especially liked.

"This is kind of like the quilts we made," Danny said.

"In what way?" asked Rusty.

"All of these shapes fit together because the sides are straight," Danny explained.

Reflecting on the experience, Rusty reported, "This task was fairly simple for the students because they had explored quilting patterns earlier in the year. If I do this activity again with children who have had this prior experience, I'll ask them to choose two different shapes for their own patterns. But I know the students enjoyed the activity, and I think it was a good way to see what they remembered from earlier in the year."

Another Lesson with Third Graders

When Marilyn Burns read the book to her class of third graders, she didn't stop as Rusty had, but read the story straight through.

Dominic commented at the end of the story, "It's kind of happy and sad at the same time."

"Yeah," Ian added, "the father was happy that his son was going to do what he wanted but sad because he would miss him."

"I agree," Lori said, "but I think it's a little more happy than sad because Misha will get to see the world."

After discussing the story and illustrations, Marilyn presented the students with the opportunity to make cloak patterns of their own.

"You won't have to sew," she told them. "Instead, you'll trace shapes, cut them out of colored paper, and paste them down to make a pattern." She had duplicated onto tagboard the same shapes that Rusty had used. (See page 25.) Also, she told the children they could trace around Pattern Blocks if they preferred.

Although these third graders had explored shapes and their properties during a geometry unit earlier in the year, they hadn't had any classroom experience with quilt patterns or tessellations. Marilyn chose to use the book to offer the children the chance to investigate piecing shapes together, and she didn't limit the students to using just one shape.

"Try different shapes and see how they can fit together," she told the class. "Then choose the shapes you'll use for your pattern. Remember, the shapes you choose must fit together snugly, with no holes and no overlaps."

Marilyn noticed that the task was easier for some children than for others, both because of the variation in children's spatial experiences and their cutting and pasting skills. She listened as the children talked among themselves about what they noticed.

Annette said to Alberto, "Look, you can line squares up to make long skinny rectangles." She used squares and several sizes of rectangles for her pattern. Alberto followed her lead and also used squares and rectangles for his pattern.

Annette pieced together squares and different-size rectangles.

Loren showed Lynn her work. "Two triangles make a parallelogram," she commented. "It's a neat shape."

A bit later, Marilyn noticed that Erin was having difficulty pasting her shapes where she wanted to. Erin said to Stewart, "You have to put them perfect or it comes out wrong. This can be very frustrating." Stewart nodded sympathetically and returned to working on his pattern. Erin kept working on hers.

Jack was also having difficulty managing the shapes. Unlike Erin, however, he didn't keep at it, but spent his time snipping the shapes into random sizes. His desk was covered with bits of colored paper. Marilyn knelt by his side.

"It's too hard," Jack said. "I can't get them to go right."

"There's a kind of design you can make using all those bits and pieces," Marilyn said. "It's not a repeating pattern, but it has a name. It's called a 'crazy quilt.' Why don't you try and see if you can fit together the pieces you cut?"

This seemed to relieve Jack's frustration for the moment, and he got back to work. He didn't finish, however. The task seemed too difficult for him, and Marilyn chose not to push him.

"He just wasn't interested enough to stick with it," Marilyn reported, "and I didn't want to risk having the experience kill his interest in exploring shapes. Jack needs more experience with concrete materials before being asked to complete a project like this."

After the children finished their patterns, Marilyn had them write about what they discovered.

Annie had pieced together hexagons and two sizes of triangles. She wrote: *When I put the shaps together I saw a Cristmas tree, a Ice creme cone and a Big Big triangle.*

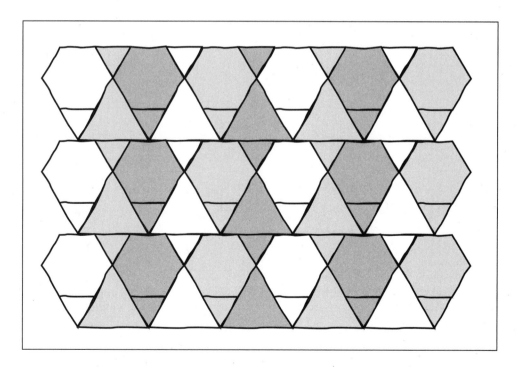

Annie saw Christmas trees and ice cream cones in her pattern.

Javier wrote: *I discovered that some shapes don't fit together.*

Seiji was more specific. He wrote: *I discovered that squares don't fit on hexegons but diamonds fit on hexegons. I discovered that 6 diamonds, 6 hexegons and 6 triangles will make a big hexegon. And I discovered 6 triangles will make a hexegon.*

Jack wrote: *Well, mine turned out not to work. It was kind of weird. Everytime I had a great idea, it never worked and the more I tried to patch it up, it made it worse.*

Daniel made a sketch of his pattern and wrote: *I had to plan it all before I did it because if I hadn't It probably wouldn't of fit together. A couple of the discoveries I made were . . . for one thing you cant cumbind a square with a hexagon. You cant even cubind a square with a diamond a traingle or* <u>veriouse</u> *other shapes.*

Daniel sketched his pattern and wrote about his discoveries.

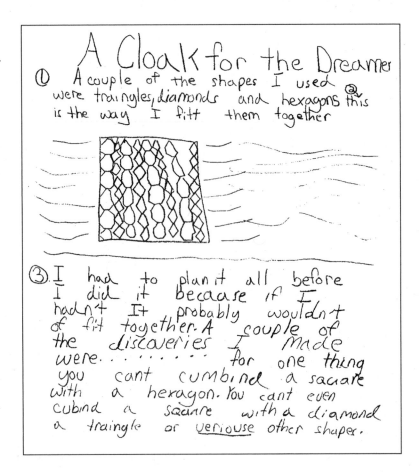

(Note: *A Cloak for the Dreamer* provides the basis for two whole class lessons and an independent "menu" activity in the replacement unit *Math By All Means: Geometry, Grades 1-2* by Chris Confer. See the bibliography for additional information.)

A Cloak for the Dreamer Shapes

The Greedy Triangle

The Greedy Triangle, by Marilyn Burns, is the story about a triangle who always wishes for more. At the beginning of the story, the triangle supports bridges, makes music in symphony orchestras, catches the wind for sailboats, and much, much more. After a while, however, the triangle becomes dissatisfied and is sure that if it had one more side and one more angle, its life would be far more interesting. The local shapeshifter grants the triangle's wish and turns it into a quadrilateral, then a pentagon, then a hexagon, and so on, until the shape finally learns that being a triangle is best after all. The story provides a springboard for first, second, and third graders to explore shapes.

I read *The Greedy Triangle* to my class of first graders during a unit on geometry. Although I had them sit on the floor around me to see the book, they kept popping up to point to the pictures. As I read the page describing how the triangle spent its time, the children studied the illustrations carefully, looking for pictures of triangles that weren't mentioned in the story.

When I read, "The triangle's favorite thing, however, was to slip into place where people put their hands on their hips," I asked Andie to stand up and put her hands on her hips so that all the children could see the triangle shape pictured in the book. Some children seemed confused, but their confusion soon ended as they took turns making triangles with their arms and tracing the shape on one another with their hands. Many students need a kinesthetic way to experience a new idea.

After reading the page where the triangle wished for one more angle and one more side, I paused. "What would the triangle look like if its wish were granted?" I asked the students.

"A square!" several students answered.

Although we had talked about the word "quadrilateral" for four-sided figures, children used the word they knew best. Eddie, however, glanced at our list of geometry words posted on the wall. He found the word "quadrilateral," but he couldn't quite pronounce it. I said it aloud and had the children repeat it.

"How many sides will the new shape have?" I asked. They all knew it would be four.

When the shape was about to make its next change, from a quadrilateral to a pentagon, I said to the children, "Close your eyes and imagine what the shape will look like now." Nina put her finger up and drew her "picture" in the air but could not articulate what it was. Craig shouted, "A house!"

As we looked at the pictures of the pentagon, I noticed that the children were less familiar with objects shaped like pentagons. I made a mental note to look for some and point them out.

Each time the shape added a side and an angle, I stopped and asked the class how many sides and angles it had. For some first graders, the question of one more is not trivial.

As I read the rest of the book, the children searched the pictures to see what the shape did each time it became a new polygon. The children seemed to sense that the triangle was headed for trouble after it had more than eight sides.

"Oh, no! He's rolling!" Nina said.

"He's turning into a circle!" yelled Cal.

The children giggled when they saw the dazed shape at the bottom of the hill. Although they had enjoyed seeing the triangle explore new shapes, the children seemed relieved when the triangle decided to return to its original shape and to the company of its friends.

After reading the book, I asked the class, "What do you think the triangle might like to do if it visited our school?" The students had many ideas to share, but rather than having them share them aloud, I asked them to wait for just a minute.

"We'll take a walk around the school to look for places that the triangle might fit into if it were here," I said.

I gave each child a small book I had made by folding newsprint and stapling it inside a construction paper cover. Then I gave directions. "When you spot a place the triangle might fit," I said, "first check with your partner to be sure you both agree that it's the shape of a triangle. Then each of you should draw in your booklet a picture of what you saw. Be sure to draw the triangle's face so that others will understand your idea."

I had the children line up in pairs and we set out on our walk. We went to the playground first. The students spied triangles everywhere. Mary and Sharon ran immediately to the swing set and began sketching the triangle they saw connecting the rubber seat to the chain that held it.

Mary and Sharon
found a triangle on
the swing set.

we fownd
a trlYangle
ona sweg

Craig and Anita climbed the steps leading to the suspended bridge and sat down to draw. Some pairs had difficulty staying together as they searched, but I reminded them that they needed to check with their partners before drawing.

Ronnie and Kimberly ran up to show me their first drawing. I could tell from Kimberly's book that they were sketching the plastic roof of the climbing structure, but I had difficulty understanding Ronnie's drawing. Because I wanted to be sure that I would know what the students had drawn, and that the children would remember as well, I called the students together.

"When you find a triangle and draw it, write a few words on the page to tell what you're looking at," I told them. "We want to be able to remember where the triangle might go if it visits our school."

After spending a little more time on the playground, we continued our walk, heading toward the library, then the parent workroom, and finally through the halls. I was amazed at how many triangular shapes the students were able to spot. My reading the book had helped them think about triangles in a new way. It was as if the word "triangle" had come down from our chart of geometry words and become part of the real world.

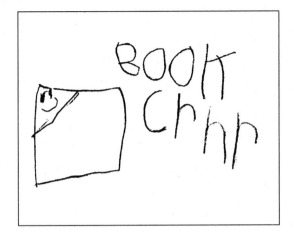

On their walk around the school, first graders found triangles on a variety of objects.

From A Second Grade Class

When I read *The Greedy Triangle* to second graders, the students listened as attentively as the first graders had. They, too, needed to try out making triangles with their hands on their hips. We had a lively discussion about the interesting places the triangle visited.

As the triangle changed to a quadrilateral, then a pentagon, and so on, I wrote the names of the shapes on the board and recorded the number of sides next to each name. I talked about the prefixes—tri-, quad-, penta-, hexa-, octa-, and so on. "What other words do you know that begin with these prefixes?" I asked. The children brainstormed words and we talked about what they meant.

When I finished reading the book, I took out a collection of triangles I had cut out of construction paper. There were many shapes and sizes, and I spread them out in front of me.

"There are enough triangles so that everyone can choose one," I told the children. "Take the triangle you choose to your desk, and turn it around to look at it from different angles. Think about what this triangle might be a part of. When you have an idea, come get a piece of white paper and glue the triangle down. Draw a picture around it to show where your triangle is and then write a sentence to describe your picture."

The children were eager to get started. Hassan began his drawing right away, sure of the picture in his mind even before I could tell what it was going to be. Some children, however, took several minutes to locate the triangle, turn it over, and really think about it. Some watched their friends and borrowed ideas from others at their tables.

The results were varied. Scott pictured his triangle as part of the pleated skirt of a cheerleader. Reed drew it as the beak of a penguin. Antonio's triangle became an escalator in a department store. Judy drew a pennant in a girl's hand.

It's important for children to understand that geometry is a part of the world around them, and this book helped children make this connection. Also, integrating art and mathematics is an effective way to help children develop their spatial reasoning.

Two days after I visited this class, I saw Scott in the hall. "Hi, Mrs. Sheffield," he said. Then he added, "You're the one who brings the neat math books! When are you coming back again?"

(Note: In the replacement unit *Math By All Means: Geometry, Grades 3-4*, by Cheryl Rectanus, *The Greedy Triangle* provides the basis for a whole class lesson in which students rewrite and illustrate the story. See the bibliography for more information.)

Reed wrote: *My pictur is a penguin the triangle is the beak.*

Scott wrote: *This is his favorit thing to do stick on a cheerleader skirt.*

Janine wrote: *This is a slide that children can play on in the summer time.*

The House

The House is a part of a series of mouse books by Monique Felix. This wordless book features a delicately drawn mouse. As he sits alone on a sheet of white paper, he pokes a small hole in the paper, chews to make it big enough to stick his head through, and disappears through the hole, only to reappear on the next page. The mouse continues to chew and finally folds the paper to make a house. The book leads to a lesson that gives kindergarten children experience thinking spatially and using geometric vocabulary, as they describe how to fold a paper square to make a house as the mouse did. Older children can tackle folding their own houses.

I read this book to a kindergarten class near the end of the school year. I told the children that this book didn't have any words.

"What will we do?" I asked. "How will we understand the story if there are no words?"

"We'll have to use our imagination," said Lori.

"We can read the pictures!" exclaimed Natalya.

"Let's try the first page," I said. "Who can look at the picture and imagine what is happening?"

Victoria said, "The mouse is sad."

On the next page, Isaac said, "He's biting it!"

"Look, grass!" Lori added.

"He's making a heart," Saul noticed.

As the mouse began to chew lines in the paper to build the house, Winnie noticed that the lines made a shape that looked like an "E."

"It's a backwards E," Peymen corrected her, and then turned to me. "Turn the book around," he directed. "Now it's right, but the mouse is upside down." He giggled.

When I showed the next page, Amber commented, "He's making a square with lines in the sides."

"I think he's making a house!" Saul said.

"Could it be a trailer house?" asked Natalya.

"He's folding the paper," said Abby.

And finally, Amber said, "He *is* making a house!"

Creating words for the book engaged the children and helped them connect with the story. When we finished reading, I made a suggestion to the class.

"How about helping me make a house from paper?" I asked. The children were excited about the idea.

"What shape did the mouse start with?" I asked.

"A square," Peymen said.

"Yes," I agreed, and showed them an 8-inch square of paper.

"What do you know about a square?" I asked.

"It has four sides," said Brandy.

"It has four corners too," Victoria said.

Asking questions such as these was a valuable part of the lesson. The children's answers helped me to understand what they knew about the properties of shapes and the vocabulary of geometry. Children who were unfamiliar with the shapes and words had a chance to hear them used in a context.

"What should I do next?" I asked.

"You have to cut the paper," Abby said.

"How will I know where to cut?" I asked. This stumped the children.

"Watch as I fold the square in half," I said. "How many parts do you think there will be when I open up the paper?"

"Two," most of the children called out. I unfolded the paper to verify for the children that there were now two parts.

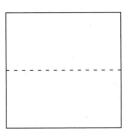

"Now I'll fold the paper again on the same crease, and then I'll fold it in half once more," I said, folding the paper as I explained. "How many parts do you think there will be now?"

The children all started talking at once. I asked for their attention. "Whisper what you think to the person next to you," I instructed them. After a moment, I opened the paper to show the four parts.

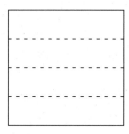

I refolded the paper on both creases and folded it in half once again. I opened it up on the second two folds, leaving the paper still half folded.

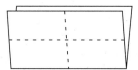

"Now how many sections do you think there will be when I open the last fold?" I asked.

"I see four," Natalya said, referring to the four sections on the half she could see. I turned the paper around so that the children could see the four sections on the other side.

"Four on one side, and four on the other," I said.

"Four plus four makes eight!" Victoria exclaimed. I opened the paper and had the children count the eight sections.

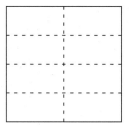

I folded the paper back and then once more in half. Again, I had the children predict, and then I opened the paper and had them count the 16 sections.

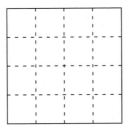

Next, I folded the paper in half and cut half of a heart shape on the fold line.

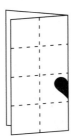

Cut half of a heart shape.

I opened the paper so the children could see the heart. Then I cut on the fold lines on two sides of the square. I held up the book for the children so they could see the page that showed these same cuts.

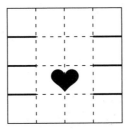

Cut on bold lines.

I turned the page and asked the children to describe how the mouse was folding the paper, but it was difficult for them to do. I showed them the next two pages to remind them what the house would look like. Then I creased the square on the center fold, over-lapped the two middle squares on the end to create a roof, and brought the two squares on the end together. I used tape to secure the side of the house.

Then I did the same on the other side to complete the house.

"Ooh, it's cute," Brandy said.

"Can we make a mouse to go in it?" Abby asked.

I focused the children on the various shapes. "What shape is this part of the roof with the heart in it?" I asked.

"That's a rectangle," Peymen said.

"Do you see other rectangles?" I asked.

"That side on the bottom," Victoria said.

"And on the back, too," Natalya added.

"What about this end of the house?" I asked, turning the house to show one end to the children.

Several children called out. "A triangle on top." "It's a triangle." "I see a square." "There's a rectangle." I asked for the students' attention and talked about the shapes they noticed.

"Where do you see a triangle, Amanda?" I asked. Amanda pointed to the triangular shape I created when I overlapped the two square flaps.

"You can't see it until you tape the sides down," Eddie added.

"Then the other two squares make a rectangle," Lamar noticed.

"What shape is the front of the house?" I asked.

"It's a rectangle too!" Sandi exclaimed.

I held my house up and pointed to the roof. "I see two shapes coming together at the top to make this roof. What shapes are these?" I turned the house several times so students could see it from different perspectives.

Megan said, "Oh, yeah, I see two rectangles!" She came up and traced the shapes to show the others.

From a First Grade Class

I read this book to my first graders in much the same way as I had to the kindergarten class. But instead of my making a house with them watching, I had them all make their own. After sharing the book, I showed the children the page in the book where the mouse has almost finished nibbling the lines for the house. I had made a transparency of this page to use later.

"What do you think we need to know to make a house of our own?" I asked.

Eddie responded, "It's a square shape to start with."

"That's right, Eddie, and I've cut squares of construction paper for you to use," I said. I stopped and passed out the paper. "What else do you see?"

Mary said, "He chewed the paper in straight lines."

"We'll do that too, but we'll cut with scissors instead of chewing. How many lines do we need to cut?" I asked.

Conner pointed toward the illustration as he counted. He raised his hand. "There's three on each side, six altogether," he said.

Reggie added, "All the cuts are the same."

"How far in do the cuts go?" I asked.

"Halfway," Lori answered.

"No, not that far," said Reggie.

I displayed the transparency and folded it so that the lines on the sides of the house were on top of one another. Now we could see that the cuts went halfway to the center on each side.

"How will we know where to cut the lines so that they go halfway to the center?" I asked. The children looked puzzled.

"Could we fold the paper in half?" Lamar asked.

"That's a good start," I said. "Fold your paper in half, matching the corners carefully." I said. I walked around, assisting children who needed help. Matching corners and making folds is still difficult for many first graders, even late in the year.

"Now to find out where halfway to the center is, we'll have to fold again." I held my paper up against the chalkboard and showed them how to fold the square again. I opened the square.

"This shows us how far we need to cut, but now we need straight lines to cut on," I said. I showed the children how to fold the paper twice again, this time making folds perpendicular to the others. I encouraged the children to watch me. For some children, folding was very difficult. Justin needed help with almost all his folds. But Alexandra had done some origami this year and found it easy.

Next, we identified where the little heart should go. We counted the squares to find the right spot. It needed to be right in the middle, two rows from the bottom. I reminded the class about the symmetry lesson we had done earlier in the year when we learned how to cut a heart from a folded sheet of paper. "Remember, the fold will be the line of symmetry, so you'll only draw half of the heart," I said. "Everyone cut a little heart out of the center of the paper."

When we began to attach the flaps of the roof together with glue, I was struck by the difficulty I had explaining how to do this. As clear as I thought my directions were, some children had to watch me up close to understand. As the children experimented, their houses began to take shape, and I heard the sound of satisfaction in their voices.

"Look, it's really a house!" Colleen said.

Making this house was a challenge for many of the children. But I believe that children need many kinds of opportunities to develop their spatial reasoning skills. The problem solving and visualizing were valuable, and the children were delighted with the little houses they took home that day.

The King's Commissioners

Hilarious pictures complement this tale by Aileen Friedman about a King who has so many commissioners he loses track of how many there are. The King tells his commissioners to file into the throne room to be counted by his two Royal Advisors. One Royal Advisor counts by 2s, and the other counts by 5s, but the King is confused. It's up to the clever Princess to convince her father that there is more than one way to count. The book suggests a lesson that helps first, second, and third graders think about place value.

I read this book to first graders near the end of the year when they were beginning to work with the concept of place value. I began by showing the children the cover of the book.

"Who knows what a commissioner is?" I asked.

"Some kind of helper?" Ross said tentatively.

Monique said, "I think it's like a fairy."

"You're both right in a way," I responded. "A commissioner is someone who helps the King with important matters. This is the King on the front cover. How does it look like he feels?"

Jane responded, "Mad!"

"No, I think he looks confused," Ben disagreed.

"Let's read and find out," I said. I read the first page aloud: "The King was confused."

"I was right!" Ben exclaimed.

"Look at the clocks!" Mary said. "One is ringing but the others aren't."

Ahmed jumped up. "I know why the King is confused! All the clocks tell a different time!"

"It looks as if he really does have a problem," I said, and I continued reading. A few minutes later Lamar waved his hand wildly, rocking back and forth on his heels. I stopped reading and called on him.

"I know why the clocks all had a different time maybe," he said. "They could all be made in different places, and the times could be from the places the clocks were made."

"That's an interesting idea, Lamar," I said. I called on Lamar because I wasn't sure he would have been able to concentrate on the story if he hadn't had the chance to share his idea.

The children were interested and involved as I read the story, and they made many comments about the plot and illustrations. When the King decides to line up the commissioners and count them one by one, Barbara said, "That's a good idea. That way he won't miss any of them."

I turned the page. "Look at those swans blowing trumpets!" Greg exclaimed. The children were delighted by the bright, expressive pictures and commented on them throughout the book.

When I read the First Royal Advisor's explanation of his method of counting by 2s, some of the children started to figure. Conner started counting by 2s, trying to keep track on his fingers of how far he had counted.

"It's 51," Greg whispered to Bonnie. I kept reading.

On the next page, the Second Royal Advisor shows his tally system to the King. I saw several children counting on their fingers again. Although they were intrigued, I knew I would give them time to think about the numbers a little later, so I read on.

As soon as the King orders the Royal Commissioners arranged in rows of 10s, Conner exclaimed, "That's 47!" And when the Princess counts by 10s to 40 to explain to the King why the advisors were right, the whole class counted aloud.

At the end of the story, the King and the First Royal Advisor say that they need a Commissioner to Keep Count of the Royal Commissioners. "That makes 48!" Barbara stated. The King suggests that the Princess would be a likely candidate for this job if she weren't in school.

"Hey, princesses don't go to school," Conner protested.

"Everybody has to go to school," Jane said.

I called for the students' attention. "Who remembers how the First Royal Advisor counted the commissioners?" I asked. I called on Jeremy.

"He counted by 2s and added 1 more," he said. On the board I recorded: *23 2s and 1 more*.

"Who can explain why his way to count made sense?" I asked.

"I think he's right because 3 and 3 is 6 and 2 and 2 is 4 and 1 more is 47," Bill said.

"Can you come to the board and show us what you mean?" I asked.

Bill wrote two 23s, one under the other, and showed how he added to get 46.

"Can you tell us why you added 23 and 23?" I asked. Bill thought for a moment and said, "I don't know why, but I just think it's right." Bill has a strong intuitive feel for numbers. Adding two 23s made sense to him, but he couldn't verbalize why. I recorded *two 23s* on the board.

I then asked, "Can someone else explain why the First Advisor's method makes sense?"

Jane raised her hand. "If you look at the picture of the First Advisor," she said, "you can count his circles by 2s and you get to 46. Then you add the one that doesn't have a circle and that makes 47." I saw heads nod as other children agreed with Jane's thinking.

"What about the Second Royal Advisor's counting plan? Does it make sense?" I asked. I looked around for a child who hadn't shared much yet. Jeremy had raised his hand.

"I think I know what he did," he said.

"Can you explain what you think?" I asked.

"Because 9 times 5 is 45," Jeremy said, "and 2 more makes 47." Jeremy has great facility with numbers.

"I'll record what you said so we can all look at it," I said. "Would you say that again, Jeremy?"

As he spoke, I wrote on the board: $9 \times 5 + 2 = 47$. "Jeremy is right," I told the class. "Nine groups of 5 and 2 more make 47." I knew that most of the class didn't have a clue about Jeremy's use of multiplication, but it was perfectly clear to Jeremy. I didn't expand any further on his explanation.

"Does anyone else have an idea about why the Second Royal Advisor's method of counting makes sense?" I asked.

Jolie responded, "It's like adding 5 plus 5 plus 5 plus 5 . . . if you do that nine times you get 45, and 2 more is 47." I recorded Jolie's idea: $5 + 5 + 5 + 5 + 5 + 5 + 5 + 5 + 5 = 45 + 2 = 47$. I had the children count aloud by 5s and then count 2 more to verify the answer.

No other children had ideas, so I moved on to something else. "After the King knew there were 47 commissioners," I said, "he decided that wasn't so many after all. Maybe we could come up with a few more commissioners for the King. Remember, a commissioner gets named when there is a problem that the King needs help with. If I could name a new commissioner, I would make a Commissioner for Messy Desks."

"You really need one of those!" Paul commented. The whole class giggled; the children are well acquainted with the typical confusion on my desk.

I continued. "We all have some little problem in our lives that we wish someone else would take care of for us. I want you to think of problems you have and come up with commissioners to take care of them. Figure out how many commissioners the King would have if he appointed all the ones you suggest. Then show how the Princess would count them. Who remembers how she arranged them to count?" I asked.

Monique said, "She put them in rows of 10 and counted by 10s."

"That's right," I said. "I'd like you to make groups of 10 and extras and tell how many commissioners there are in all."

I wrote the directions on the board:

1. *Name new commissioners.*
2. *How many commissioners would the King have altogether if he had yours and his?*

Rudy asked for seven commissioners, then counted on from 47 to get a total of 54.

As the children worked, I walked around and observed them. I noticed who had fun and who had difficulty thinking up commissioners. When I read Ross's paper, I knew I was getting a glimpse at his seven-year-old life. He wrote: *Comishner for keeping my lite sister away from my art work. Comishner for eating my brekfast because I don't like it. Comishner for ordering me pizza with only cheese. Comishner for buying me cake not on my birthday.*

Monique was a little more practical. She wrote: *A cuomitinshner to help me ahding,* and *A cuomitinshner for when you don't no wuhe't* [what] *to give sumeone on thear birthday.*

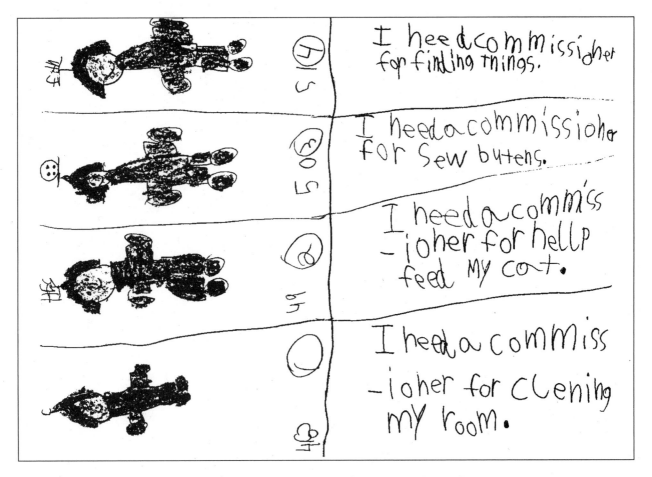

I heed a commissioher for finding things.

I heed a commissioher for sew butens.

I heed a commiss-ioher for hellp feed my cot.

I heed a commiss-ioher for clening my room.

Molly carefully illustrated her four commissioners, even including a hat for each one.

To decide how many commissioners the King would have in all, Greg counted on from 47 to 51. Kitty made tally marks, circled groups of 10, and wrote the number sentence: *47 + 10 = 57*. Penny drew pictures of three smiling figures. She named them and described the housework each would do for her. She counted on from 47 to 50, recorded 50 on her paper, and circled it. Jolie was the most prolific of the class. She thought of 25 additional commissioners. She made tally marks to count them, circling groups of 10 and counting the extras.

Lamar thought of four commissioners for himself and used tally marks to find the total number of commissioners.

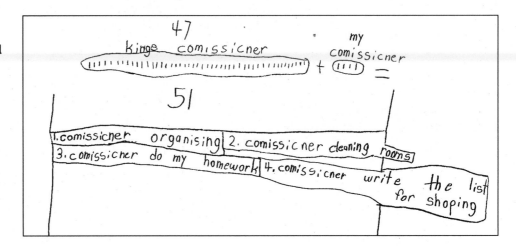

This lesson presented the students with different ways to count, and showed how you can get the same number if you count in different ways. One of my favorite things about this book is that there is something in it for everyone. Children can become intrigued with why the clocks are all telling a different time, imagine a houseful of helpers, or struggle to add 47 + 8. This book is rich mathematically, and it engages students with varying abilities.

From Second and Third Grade Classes

Marilyn Burns read the book to second graders near the middle of the year when they were studying place value and also to third graders at the beginning of the year. In both situations, after reading the story, she presented the students with two problems. First, she asked them to write about why the Royal Advisors' and Princess's methods made sense. She wrote a prompt on the board to structure the students' writing:

1. *The First Royal Advisor made sense because . . .*
2. *The Second Royal Advisor made sense because . . .*
3. *The Princess made sense because . . .*

47 commissioners

The fisrt royal Advisor made sense because you go 2 4 6 8 10 246810 246810 246810 2467 and you count the 246810s and you will get to 4 that means 40 than you add the 7 and it is 47

the second royal advisor made sense because you go 5 10 15 20 25 30 35 40 45 plus 2 more makes 47

the prinsses made sense because you go 10 20 30 40 plus 7 is 47

Annette explained how to count by 2s, 5s, and 10s. She included an illustration of the Princess.

She also asked the students to think about how many more commissioners the King might need and how many he would have in all. She asked them to explain how the two Royal Advisors and the Princess would figure the total. Marilyn reported that the activity went well in both situations.

(Note: Marilyn's experience with second graders is described more fully in *Math By All Means: Place Value, Grades 1–2.* See the bibliography for additional information.)

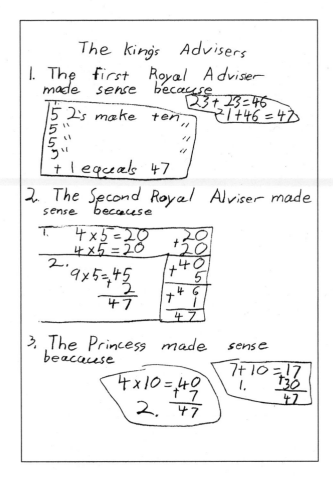

Alex calculated in several ways.

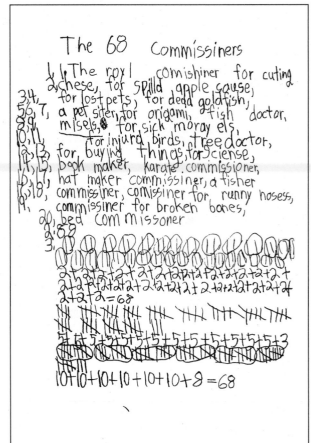

Jamshid counted 68 commissioners in all.

Mrs. Fitz's Flamingos

> *Mrs. Fitz's Flamingos*, by Kevin McCloskey, tells the story of Mrs. Fitz, who buys two pink plastic flamingos for $3.00 and ties them to the railing of her fire escape. She likes them so much that she buys more, adding a new pair each week. She eventually moves her collection to the rooftop of the warehouse next door. One day she sees a wrecking ball poised to demolish the warehouse, and she rushes to save the flamingos. The story resolves with a magical ending, as the flamingos come to life, stretch their wings, and fly away. The story provides the context for engaging children with numerical problems that can be solved in a variety of ways.

Before I read this book aloud to second graders, I held it up and showed both sides of the cover. I asked the students where they thought the story took place.

Reed answered, "It looks like New York."

"What makes you say that?" I asked.

"You can tell it's a city, and I can see a bridge on the cover," he said.

Antonio added, "She's in an apartment building."

A few pages into the story, after hearing that Mrs. Fitz bought her first pair of flamingos for $3.00, Judy called out, "That's a dollar fifty each." I made a mental note of how comfortably Judy divided this amount in half.

When I read the page where Mrs. Fitz had 12 flamingos, I stopped. "How many pairs did she buy?" I asked. Many hands shot up in the air.

"Let's say it together," I said.

"Six!" shouted the students. Together we looked at the pictures of the dozen flamingos first on the fire escape, then in Mrs. Fitz's apartment, and finally on the warehouse roof.

Jane commented, "It doesn't look like so many on the roof."

"Why do you think that's so?" I asked.

Karen said, "When they were in the apartment, they were all scrunched up and now they're spread out."

As we turned the page to find the roof covered with many more flamingos, the class broke out in exclamations of amazement. "There must be a hundred now!" Kendra said. Jed began to try to count them from his place on the floor.

When I read about Mrs. Fitz's race to save her flamingos when the warehouse was about to be demolished, the students' eyes got bigger and bigger. And when the flamingos spread their wings and began to fly, there were exclamations of disbelief and surprise.

This sudden shift from reality to fantasy was a little hard for some of the children to accept. We spent some time talking about the book and discussing what changed the flamingos at the end. "It's like the Velveteen Rabbit. Mrs. Fitz's love turned the flamingos real," Judy commented.

After our discussion, I said to the children, "I've thought of three problems for you to solve. Here's the first one. The story says that Mrs. Fitz bought a pair of flamingos each week. If she did this for a whole year, how many flamingos would she have?" I gave the children a few seconds for the question to sink in. Then I asked, "What do you need to know to solve this problem?"

Mark asked, "How many weeks are there in a year?" I turned to the students and passed the question on to them.

Janine said, "I think it's 50, or something like that."

"No, it's 52," said Jed.

"Yeah, it's 52!" Antonio agreed. I saw heads nodding around the room in agreement.

"Here's the second problem," I said. "When Mrs. Fitz had to bring her flamingos in from the fire escape, she had 12 of them. If she bought them for $3.00 a pair, how much did she spend for all 12?"

Debbie raised her hand. "Do they cost $3.00 for one or $3.00 for two?"

"What does '$3.00 a pair' mean?" Kendra asked.

"A pair means two, so it's $3.00 for two." I said. There were no other questions.

"Here's the third problem," I said. "If Mrs. Fitz bought a pair of flamingos every week, how much money would she spend in a year?" I reviewed the three problems and wrote them on the board:

1. *If Mrs. Fitz bought one pair each week, how many flamingos would she have in a year?*
2. *If flamingos cost $3.00 a pair, how much did Mrs. Fitz spend for 12 flamingos?*
3. *How much would Mrs. Fitz spend in a year?*

"Does anyone have questions before you begin?" Since no one raised a hand, I had the children choose partners or choose to work alone.

The first question seemed interesting and accessible to all the students. Audrey and Debbie started by drawing two small circles with a ring around them. They continued drawing circles in sets of two, counting by 2s as they did so. They recorded 104 as their answer.

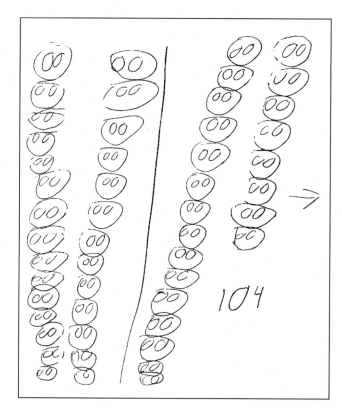

Audrey and Debbie drew pairs of small circles and counted by 2s to determine how many flamingos Mrs. Fitz bought in a year.

Judy and Antonio had written: *52 + 52 = 104*. They then felt ready to go on to the next problem. I interrupted them.

"Why did you add 52 and 52?" I asked.

Judy said, "Because 52 would be only one flamingo, but she bought them in pairs, so you have to add it twice."

"Write that down to explain the arithmetic you did," I said. I left them and they wrote: *A pair is two if you add 52 & 52 that equals 104.*

Scott also got the correct answer. He wrote: *I drew 2 tally marks and circled. Then I counted by twos.*

Scott used tally marks and carefully counted each pair.

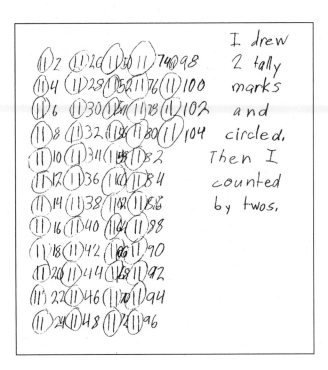

From Jane and Angie: *We think it is 104 flamingoes because we added 52 plus 52. And came up with 104.*

To explain their answer for the second question about the 12 flamingos, Janine and Karen drew six groups of two tally marks each. They figured out that the 12 flamingos cost $18.00.

To answer question number two, Janine and Karen counted by 3s, concluding that Mrs. Fitz paid $18.00 for 12 flamingos.

Jane and Angie, however, wrote: *We added 3.00 12 times because she bought 12 pairs of flamingos and they cost 3.00 dollars for a pair.* Other students also made this error of figuring out the cost of 12 pairs instead of 12 flamingos.

To answer the third question of how much Mrs. Fitz spent in a year, Audrey and Debbie added 52 three times and got 156. To explain, they drew three large circles and put 52 marks inside each. They wrote: *52 + 52 + 52 = 156.*

Jane and Angie wrote: *We added 52 three times because each pair cost $3.00 each and there are 52 weeks in a year.*

Jane and Angie explained clearly how they reached their answer.

Janine and Karen counted by 3s, recording each number as they said it aloud. They numbered these results as they went, so they would know when they got to 52.

Scott worked as Janine and Karen had, counting by 3s to keep track. Although Scott's approach was correct, he made two counting errors and wound up with the wrong answer. He wrote: *I counted by threes and then I numbered them up and got $126. That's how I did it.*

Some students spent a lot of time working on the last problem, while others finished more quickly. When all the children were finished, I gathered them on the rug. I asked Janine and Karen if they would like to share first. I knew they had counted to find their answer to the last problem, and I wanted to validate counting as a strategy. I was afraid that if Janine and Karen saw that others had multiplied to get the answer, they would think that their own solution was somehow not as good.

I gave all pairs of children the opportunity to share their work. I think it's important for students to hear as many different solutions to a problem as possible. Although the children were finished with this problem, they might use the ideas they heard the next time they worked on a similar problem.

Musical Chairs and Dancing Bears

> *Musical Chairs and Dancing Bears*, by Joanne Rocklin, takes place at a birthday party. Ten little bears are playing musical chairs. The music changes as each round begins, from waltz to rock and roll, to polka and square dance, and more. Each time the music stops, the bears scramble for chairs, and one bear is left standing. The story counts down until only one bear is left, and then the game begins again. The book is ideal for giving kindergartners experiences with counting down from 10 and thinking about the ideas of "one more" and "one less."

I showed the book to a class of kindergarten students, and together we looked at the cover and the title.

"They're having a party!" Marlon said.

"They're going around the chairs," Winnie observed.

"I know what they're doing," Bobbie said. She went on to explain, with the help of her classmates, how to play musical chairs. Then I read the title and the author's name aloud.

"The title rhymes—bears and chairs!" Amber said.

As I read the story aloud, the children participated in the reading by chiming in on each page. I read the words on the first two pages, and together we counted the bears seated in chairs. After the rock-and-roll dance, Victoria said, "That makes eight and one on the ground. That's nine!"

About halfway through the book, the children noticed the small black-and-white drawings of bears on one side of a page and chairs on the other side. The pictures correspond to the words on the page. "Six dancing bears—only five chairs," said Marlon.

When we turned the page, we counted the bears sitting in chairs. "Six bears in chairs," I said. "And one more standing. How many bears in all?" Bobbie stood up and started to count them. She didn't count on as Victoria had earlier, but counted all of the bears, one by one.

I turned the page to continue reading. Abby said, "Five dancing bears—only four chairs."

"How did you know what would come next?" I asked.

Marlon answered, "It's because we're going backwards."

"Let's count backwards from 10," I said. We started out slowly. "10, 9, 8, 7, 6," we said. The closer we got to 1, the stronger and more confident their voices became. Children need a good deal of practice in order to learn to count backwards. Knowing how to count backwards doesn't come automatically; familiarity with counting forward isn't necessarily sufficient. (Have you tried saying the alphabet backwards?)

As I read the next page, Natalya held up three fingers. She said, "Three in chairs and one on the floor, that makes four!" The smaller numbers were much easier for the children to deal with.

On the last page I asked, "How many bears do you think are on this page?"

Amber answered, "Ten, because they're all together now, since it's the end."

This was a fun book to share with kindergartners. They loved the party atmosphere of the pictures and enjoyed chiming in when we read, "__ dancing bears, only ___ chairs." The lesson gave me the opportunity to assess children's ability to count backwards, add 1 to a number, and subtract 1. Also, the book gave children practice with counting and using a pattern to make predictions.

The Napping House

> *The Napping House*, by Audrey Wood, is a beautifully illustrated book about a house full of napping inhabitants. The story begins with a granny snoring away on a dark and rainy day. One by one, she is joined in bed by a dreaming child, a dozing dog, a snoozing cat, a slumbering mouse, and finally, a wakeful flea. This last arrival begins a chain reaction that results in the whole group awakening just as the rain stops and the sun comes out. The story leads to a numerical problem-solving experience for which there are multiple answers.

As soon as I put the big book on the easel, I heard exclamations of recognition from the first graders.

"I remember that from kindergarten," Harlan said.

"This is a good book," Reggie added.

I didn't mind that the children were familiar with the book. Any good book is worth reading many times, and I planned to extend the story into a math activity.

After reading the book, I asked the children if they could describe something in the book that changed gradually. I noticed a couple of quizzical looks, so I asked, "Who knows what I mean by 'gradual'?"

Mark responded, "Does it mean a little at a time?"

"Yes," I answered. "When something changes gradually, it changes slowly over time, rather than suddenly or all at once."

Colleen raised her hand now. "At the beginning of the book, everything is dark, and at the end it's light."

"Did that happen a little at a time or all at once?" I asked. We checked the illustrations to confirm that it was a gradual change.

Lamar answered next. "The bed went downer and downer when everybody was on it." We returned to the book to look at the sagging mattress.

Next Maureen noticed that the rain stopped gradually as the sleepers woke up. Then Mary pointed out that characters began leaving the bed after the wakeful flea arrived.

I posed a question. "When all the sleepers were piled up, how many feet were in the bed?" I suggested that we make a list of the characters in the story as a way to answer this question. As the class recalled the characters, I recorded them on the board, along with the number of feet each one had.

a snoring granny	2
a dreaming child	2
a dozing dog	4
a snoozing cat	4
a slumbering mouse	4
a wakeful flea	6

When the list was complete, some children immediately began counting on their fingers, while others seemed not to know how to figure out how many feet there were altogether. I offered a suggestion. "When I have to add a list of numbers like this, I look for pairs or groups of numbers that add up to 10. I'll show you." I drew a bracket connecting the 6 with the 4 and wrote 10 on the side. I explained what I was doing, as I put two 4s together to make 8 and added 2 to the 8 to get another 10. Now I had two 10s, and I added the 2 to the equation. Mark shouted, "22!"

a snoring granny	2 —— 2
a dreaming child	2
a dozing dog	4 > 10
a snoozing cat	4
a slumbering mouse	4 > 10
a wakeful flea	6

"Now you're each going to make a house and think about the number of feet in it." I gave each child a piece of white 8½-by-11-inch paper and demonstrated the origami folds to make a paper house, giving instructions as I folded. I took the students through the folds, one step at a time. At each step, I asked a question to help them check their work: "Does your paper look like mine?"

Below are the directions for making the paper house.

Fold the paper in half, bringing the two 8½-inch edges together. Then fold it in half again the other way.

Open the last fold. Hold the paper with the folded edge up. Then fold the outer sides into the middle fold.

Open the last two folds. Then put your finger inside one fold to separate the two parts and fold the inner part into the middle fold, making a triangle appear at the top. Crease the paper so the two parts are open and there is a triangle at the top.

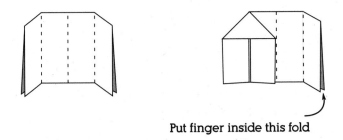

Put finger inside this fold

Do the same with the fold on the other side. The "house" should look like this:

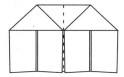

I heard exclamations of delight as the children made the final folds to create the triangles for the roof.

"It really looks like a house!" Kimberly said.

I held up my origami house and showed the children how to open the middle folds to see the inside of the house.

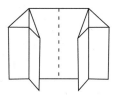

I took my marker and began to sketch as I talked. "I'm going to show you who lives in my house," I said. I drew stick figures inside my paper house to represent myself, my husband, my son, my daughter, and our cat.

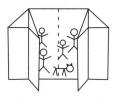

"Now let's count to find out how many feet live in my house," I said. Together we counted 12 feet. I closed the doors of the house again and wrote 12 on the outside of one of the doors.

"Since we have 12 feet living in our house, my feet number is 12," I said. "The feet number you'll write on your house will tell how many feet live inside."

I showed them my house again and said, "Did you notice that I didn't spend a lot of time drawing my pictures? This kind of drawing is called sketching. A sketch is a quickly drawn picture that doesn't have a lot of details. I'd like you to make a sketch of the people who live in your house."

Mary raised her hand. "Can I draw my dog Boris?" she asked.

"Sure," I said. "You should draw all living things that live in your house and have feet."

"Can I draw my fish?" Tom asked with a smile.

"Not unless your fish have feet," I replied.

The children began drawing, and a hush fell over the room. They were intent on their work. Even Ken, who had been wiggling and squirming through the whole lesson, was still and focused as he sketched. The connection to their own lives made this problem come alive for the children.

I walked around and observed the children working. I noticed that Timothy had written a 4 on the outside of his house. I knew that there were four people in Timothy's family.

"What does this number mean?" I asked.

"Four people in my family," he replied.

"But how many feet live in your house? Your house number needs to tell that." Timothy still looked puzzled.

"Four would be the number of feet for just you and your brother Justin," I said. "What about your Mom's and Dad's feet? You need to write the total number of feet in your house." Timothy erased the 4 and opened his house to count the feet again.

When the children had finished, I called for their attention. "Raise your hand if you think you have the smallest number of feet in your house," I said, to begin a class discussion.

Cassie raised her hand. "Mine has 10 feet," she said.

"Does anyone have a number of feet smaller than 10?" I asked.

Amy answered, "I have 12."

"Is 12 smaller than 10 or larger than 10?" I asked.

"Bigger," she answered.

"We're looking for a number that is smaller than 10," I reminded her.

Kimberly reported that she had 6 feet living in her house. "Does anyone have a number of feet that is smaller than 6?" I asked. No one did, and we agreed that 6 was the smallest number of feet living in any of our houses. I asked Kimberly to bring her house to the front of the room. I wrote the number 6 on the board and posted the house next to it. I asked other students with 6 feet in their houses to bring their houses to the front to post. We posted two more houses next to Kimberly's.

Then I asked, "Whose house might have the next larger number of feet?" Nina told us her house had 10 feet inside.

"Does anyone have a house with more than 6 feet and fewer than 10?" I asked. Around the room heads went down, as children looked at their numbers.

Alexandra said, "I have 8," and brought up her house. Brenda, Timothy, Eddie, and Carol also brought their houses up for me to post. Each had an 8 written on the outside.

"Does anyone have a number between 6 and 8?" I asked.

Maureen raised her hand. "You can't, because 7 is an odd number," she said.

"Can you explain what you mean, Maureen?" I asked.

"Legs are only even numbers," was her reply.

Mark shouted his agreement, "Legs come in twos and fours. You'd have to have a person with three legs to get seven."

I wrote an 8 on the board under the 6 and posted the five houses. "How many more houses do we have with eight feet than with six feet?" I asked. The question of how many more is difficult for many first graders. Whenever a situation comes up where comparing numbers makes sense, I try to ask this question. Children need to hear mathematical language spoken many times in order to learn to use it themselves. Also, they need to hear mathematical language used in contexts that allow them to make sense of the words.

When Lamar answered that there were two more houses with eight feet than with six feet, I asked him to explain how he figured that out. He came to the board and pointed to the two rows of houses. "These have matches on the six row," he said pointing to the first three houses next to the number 8. "These two don't have matches, so that's two more."

I continued to call children up to post their houses. We had rows marked 6, 8, 10, 12, 14, 16, 18, 20, and 24. I pointed to one house in the row marked 10.

"What could live in this house?" I asked.

"I don't know—that's not mine," Brenda said.

"Without peeking inside the doors, though, what might live in here?" I asked.

Cindy answered. As she spoke, I recorded what she said on another section of the board. "A mom, a dad, a sister, a brother,"

Cindy said and then stopped. On the board I recorded a list: *Mom—2, Dad—2, Sister—2, Brother—2.* Cindy looked at the board, her lips moving as she counted silently. Then she added, "And a baby." I added *Baby—2* to the list and had the children count together by 2s to verify that the number of feet was 10.

"Who can tell me another group of living things that could be in that house?" I asked. I called on Timothy.

"A dog," he said. I wrote: *Dog—4.* "A mom, a dad, and a cat," he added. I listed what he said, along with the number of feet for each.

"Let's add these to check," I said. I pointed to the two 4s and the class said, "8." As I pointed to the first 2, Eddie said, "Uh-oh. That's 10 and we haven't counted the dad."

"Well, we could get rid of the dad," I said, and I erased it.

Several children protested. "No, no." "Don't get rid of the dad." Apparently, I had hit a nerve. I wrote *Dad* again but accidentally put a 4 next to it instead of 2.

"Hey, dads don't have four feet!" Mary exclaimed. I replaced the 4 with a 2. Finally we decided to replace the cat with a sister.

I asked for other suggestions for the house with 10 feet. Penny offered this group: mom—2, dad—2, cat—4, and bird—2. Coleen suggested: grandma—2, parrot—2, hamster—4, and grandpa—2. I listed both of their suggestions on the board.

With four different groups of living things on the board, I asked, "Do you think this is all the ways that there could be 10 feet in this house?" Most of the class felt sure that there were more possible solutions.

"I agree that there are more solutions to this problem," I said. "But instead of continuing to work on this problem, you're going to solve one of your own. Each of you will choose one house number to investigate. You'll try to find all the different groups of living things that could live in a house with that number of feet."

I then held up a sheet of 12-by-18-inch construction paper to demonstrate how they were to organize their work. "You need to fold a sheet of paper and write each new group you think of in a separate box." I demonstrated folding the paper in half, in half again the other way, and then in half once more.

"Stop before you open the paper," I said. "How many boxes do you think there will be when the paper is open?"

Children began shouting out numbers, so I asked for quiet. I heard the numbers four, five, six, and eight.

"Whisper to the person next to you what you think," I said. Whenever I have the opportunity, I want children to think about numbers and their connections to little things the children do every day. I heard a sound of wonderment as they opened the paper and counted eight boxes.

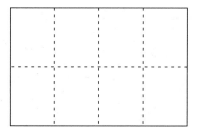

The children worked intently. Some drew pictures of families, while others made lists like the ones on the board. I noticed that some students changed the number of living things in the house as they moved from box to box on their paper. I asked for the students'

Sandi wrote lists and drew pictures of the people, animals, and insects.

attention and clarified the directions about choosing one number to explore. "Stick with one feet number for the whole page," I said. "If you choose the number 12, you need to find as many different solutions for 12 as you can."

The room was quiet as the children wrote and drew. Audrey raised her hand, and I went to her desk.

"I'm stuck," she told me.

"What's your feet number?" I asked. She pointed to the 6 on her paper.

"What can live in this house?" I asked.

"A bird," she replied.

"Write that in one box on your paper," I directed. Audrey wrote *bird* and also wrote a 2 next to it. This let me know that she basically understood the problem but just needed some reassurance that she was on the right track.

I continued asking Audrey what else lived in the house, and had her record her answers. After she completed one box, I left her to work on her own.

Alexandra found ways to show eight feet in a house.

dog 4 cat 4 [8]	bird mom 2 ses 2 me 2 [8]
dad 2 ses 2 me 2 ses [8]	causunt 2 uncle 2 dad 2 mom 2 [8]
uncle 2 mom 2 dad 2 me 2 [8]	rabeit 4 me 2 uncle 2 [8]
mom 2 dad 2 to [8] ses 4	mo m 2 me 2 dad 2 sester 2 [8]

I noticed Eddie's hand up and walked over. "I have 19 feet already, and I can't think of anything alive that has only 1 foot," he said.

"Well, Eddie," I said, "I can't think of anything with only 1 foot either. What else might be the problem?" I asked.

"Maybe I counted wrong," Eddie sighed. "I'll try again." When I looked in Eddie's direction a little while later, he smiled and gave me a thumbs-up sign. He had found and fixed his counting error.

One of my goals for students in first grade is to help them develop a sense of self-sufficiency about their problem solving. I want them to understand that they are competent mathematicians in their own right, and can verify their own answers. This problem encourages that kind of confidence. The numbers are manageable, the problem can be solved in a number of ways, and children can check their own answers in a variety of ways. I also like that children have to decide for themselves when they are finished.

Ahmed found an efficient way to find 16 feet. In many of his examples, he included a spider (8) or a flea (6).

One Hundred Hungry Ants

Eleanor J. Pinczes's book *One Hundred Hungry Ants* tells the story of 100 hungry ants hurrying to a nearby picnic. Marching in single file seems too slow to the littlest ant, who suggests they travel in two rows of 50. When that also seems too slow, the littlest ant suggests four rows of 25. The ants scurry to reorganize several more times and finally arrive at the picnic in a 10-by-10 array, too late for food! The lively marching verses delight children, and the story is useful for giving second and third graders informal experience with multiplication and division.

As I read the book aloud to a class of second graders, several of the students made comments.

"He sure is bossing them around," Reed said.

"All this stopping is slowing them down; they would get there faster if they just kept on walking," Scott commented.

"There goes the rabbit with a sandwich," Audrey noticed.

Before long, most of the students guessed that no food would be left by the time the ants got to the picnic.

After I read the book, I initiated a discussion about the different ways the littlest ant arranged his friends. "How did they start out?" I asked.

"First they were in one line of 100," Thalia said. On the board I wrote: *1 line of 100.*

"What did the littlest ant do first?" I asked. Audrey raised her hand.

"It put them in two lines of 50," she said. I recorded that as well.

Antonio started to tell me what to write next. "That made 25 rows of four," he said.

"No, that's not right. He means four rows of 25," Mark shouted.

"It's the same thing!" Hassan said. Other children called out, "No, it's not!" "Yes, it is!" The commutative nature of multiplication is a valuable concept for children to have, and the students' disagreement gave me an opportunity to help build their understanding.

"Let's think about this," I said. "How can we figure out if these two sentences are the same?" I wrote on the board: *25 rows of 4* and *4 rows of 25.*

"We could act it out," Judy suggested.

"How many children would we need?" I asked

"100!" Karen said. The children decided the idea wasn't practical. They were stumped about how to proceed.

"What makes this a hard problem?" I asked.

"We don't have enough kids to act it out," Kendra answered.

"How about a simpler problem?" I said and crossed out the 5s in the phrases so that they read *4 rows of 2* and *2 rows of 4.*

"Can you act this out?" I asked.

"Now we can do it!" Thalia said.

I called on eight students to come to an open part of the room and line up in four rows of two. As they stood there, the rest of the students walked around them and talked about what they saw.

"It's like two rows, if you walk around them," Hassan said. "I still think they're the same because it's the same eight people."

"It doesn't matter, unless they have to walk through a tunnel," Jed commented. "Then they'd better be in four rows of two."

I wasn't sure the children transferred this example to "4 rows of 25" and "25 rows of 4," but they seemed satisfied. So I had them all sit down, and we continued discussing the book. "What was the next way the littlest ant arranged its friends?" I asked.

Wally answered, "Five rows of 20. It's a pattern. One row, two rows, three rows . . . no, wait. Why didn't he put them in three rows?"

"Maybe he didn't think of it," suggested Kendra. I watched the students' faces and could tell that this was a question that intrigued them.

"I don't think it would work," said Karen.

When I chose this book to use with my class, I intended to try what Marilyn Burns reported she did with second graders. After reading the book, she asked students to choose a new number of ants and think about all the ways they could arrange themselves into rectangles to get to the picnic. She gave them a choice of numbers of ants to consider—12, 24, or 48. I had planned to do this as well.

However, because of the responses to Wally's question, I changed my plan. I've learned that what I plan for a lesson might not be what actually occurs. While it's important to have some idea about the mathematical potential in a book and plan for a lesson, it's also important to stay flexible and follow children's leads when they offer the opportunity for looking at a mathematical idea. I decided to pose a problem based on Wally's question and see what the students would do with the problem of dividing 100 into three equal groups.

"Could the littlest ant have arranged its friends into three equal lines?" I asked. "I'd like you to try to answer that question and write down your solution. If you decide the answer is yes, tell me how many ants would be in each line. If your answer is no, explain why it isn't possible. I want you to explain your thinking as clearly as possible so that someone reading your paper will know just what you were thinking. Don't worry about erasing parts that don't work out. I'm interested in all of your thinking, including your mistakes. You can use words, pictures, numbers, or any combination of these to solve the problem."

Whenever I give directions about a problem to solve, I ask several students to repeat them. This gives me a way to be sure they understand what to do. It also provides those students who are not strong in auditory skills another chance to get the directions.

"Okay, who can explain in your own words what to do?" I asked.

Reed explained, "The littlest ant wants to know if he can put all 100 ants into three rows with no leftovers. We have to tell if he can do that or not."

"Who has another way to explain the problem?" I asked.

"You have to line up 100 ants in three lines," Judy said.

"Anything else?" I prompted.

"We have to write down everything we think," Karen added.

"And we can draw pictures," Audrey said.

Some children chose partners, while others chose to work alone. Wally and Hassan made 100 tally marks, then drew a box and divided it into three parts. They transferred the 100 tally marks to the box, carefully writing them one by one in each section and crossing them off as they did so. Other students, such as Jed and Thalia, made tally marks in groups of three, counted to 100, and found there was one extra tally.

Alex and Jake started with marks in groups of three but quickly moved to writing addition problems to see if they could get to 100 by adding a number to itself three times. They started with 30 + 30 + 30 = 90, then tried 32 + 32 + 32 = 96, 33 + 33 + 33 = 99, and finally 34 + 34 + 34 = 102. At this point, they decided it was impossible and wrote 34 + 33 + 33 = 100 to prove their thinking.

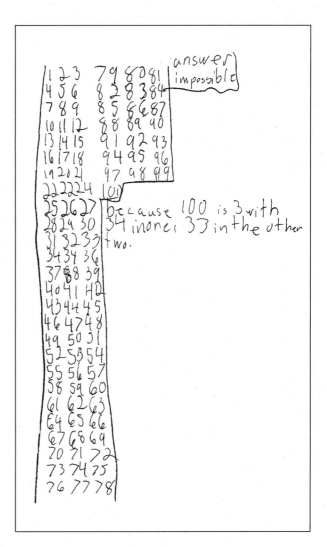

first we tried this ↓

1st

$\frac{\times 12}{36}$ 3)12
   26)12
   26)12
   26)12
   26)12

2nd Then this

$$\begin{array}{r} 30 \\ 30 \\ +30 \\ \hline 90 \end{array}$$

3rd Then

$$\begin{array}{r} 32 \\ 32 \\ +32 \\ \hline 96 \end{array}$$

4th After that

$$\begin{array}{r} 33 \\ 33 \\ +33 \\ \hline 99 \end{array}$$

5th Then

$$\begin{array}{r} 34 \\ 34 \\ +34 \\ \hline \end{array}$$

last Then we tried

$$\begin{array}{r} 34 \\ 33 \\ +33 \\ \hline 100 \end{array}$$

And that's how we knew it was impossible.

answer impossible

because 100 is 3 with 34 in one, 33 in the other two.

Alex and Jake tried adding a number to itself three times to get to 100.

Reed found the "answer impossible" after writing the numerals from 1 to 100 in columns of three.

Audrey, Angie, and Jane each made long lines of three marks to resemble the ants, while counting to 100. They knew it was impossible when the lines didn't come out even.

Reed wrote the numbers from 1 to 100, arranging them in three columns. He wound up with 100 as an extra in the first column.

As students shared their solutions, they listened to one another and seemed interested in the ways others had solved the problem. They were all convinced by their own solutions that it wasn't possible, but hearing other approaches helped to verify their thinking and introduce them to other approaches.

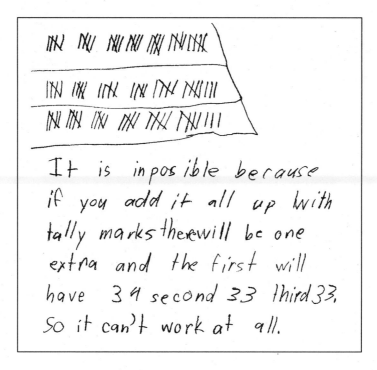

After using tally marks, Scott explained why the problem was impossible.

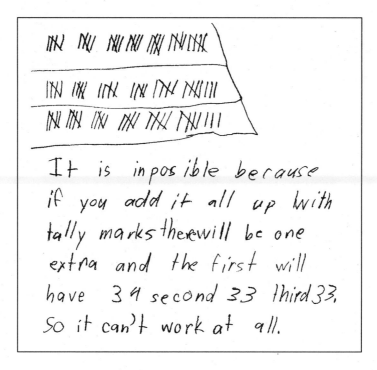

It is inposible because if you add it all up with tally marks there will be one extra and the first will have 34 second 33 third 33. So it can't work at all.

A Different Lesson with Second Graders

When Marilyn Burns used the book with second graders, she reported that after reading the story a few times, she posed a problem: "Suppose only 10 ants were going to the picnic." Marilyn drew a row of 10 circles on the board. "If the ants reorganized into two rows, how many would be in each row?" she asked. This problem was easy for the children, and Marilyn drew two lines with five dots in each to illustrate the answer.

"What about if the ants tried to get into three rows?" Marilyn then asked. "Could they get into three rows and have the same number in each?" Even though she hadn't talked about having the same number of ants in each row, the children seemed to infer this constraint from the story.

"Maybe there would be just four in each row," Leilani volunteered.

Marilyn tested Leilani's suggestion, drawing three rows with four dots in each. The children counted, found there were 12 dots in all, and agreed it wouldn't work. "Three groups of four make 12," Marilyn said and wrote *3 × 4 = 12* next to her drawing. Marilyn reported that recording like this is the sort of incidental way she tries to connect mathematical symbolism to children's thinking.

"Put three in each," Ross suggested next. Marilyn drew three rows, each with three dots.

"That's not enough," Alex said impatiently. "It won't work." Alex has a keen number sense. Marilyn had the children count the dots and recorded on the board: $3 \times 3 = 9$.

"Alex is right," she said. "You can't put 10 ants into three rows and have the same number in each row. What about four rows?" She investigated this idea with the class in the same way, drawing and labeling, to verify that it wasn't possible. Then they tried five rows and saw that it worked with two in each.

Marilyn stopped and wrote a chart on the board:

10 Hungry Ants

1 row	*10*
2 rows	*5*
3 rows	*can't*
4 rows	*can't*
5 rows	*2*
6 rows	
7 rows	
8 rows	
9 rows	
10 rows	

"A chart like this is one way to keep track of what we're finding," she told the class. "But instead of finishing this problem together, you're each going to try one on your own."

Marilyn gave the children directions. "First, decide the number of ants you'd like to explore," she said. "Then set up a chart as I did, but write your number in the title where I wrote '10.'" She erased the 10, replaced it with a dash, and erased the answers she had written so far.

"You can choose one of these numbers," Marilyn continued and wrote *12, 24,* and *60* on the board. "I like giving students options like this," Marilyn reported, "because their choices give me insights into their comfort with numbers. But I also wanted to have several children working on the same number so we could have group discussions about the results."

"Can we pick our own number?" Seiji asked. Seiji is fascinated by large numbers.

"If you want to choose a number that is different from one of these three," Marilyn responded, "then you have to tell me first, and I'll let you know if it's okay." This decision gave her the chance to converse with children about their thinking.

```
 24  Hungry    Ants
| row 24
2 row 12
3 row 8
4 row 6
5 row 4
6 row 4
8 row 3
```

I ues my Bran and
Tills

Emily used tiles to figure out the solutions.

During the rest of the math period, children set up their papers and negotiated number choices with Marilyn. Alex wanted to explore 500, and she readily agreed. Seiji asked for 200, and she told him that was fine.

David, Sheryl, and Sally were at the same table. "Can we all do 50?" they asked. Marilyn agreed, thinking they could relate this number to the story of 100 ants. Jane, also at their table, was already beginning work on 60.

When Marilyn looked at the students' papers, she noticed that of the 24 children in the class, five chose to explore 12, eight chose 24, three chose 60, and six had negotiated other choices. Two children, Lynn and Darius, had chosen their own numbers—15 and 30.

Most of the children didn't have time to finish working on the problem. The next day Marilyn reviewed the activity and had the students return to work. Three children changed their numbers; two of them changed from 24 to 12, and one changed from 60 to 12. "Changing their minds was fine with me," Marilyn reported. "I was pleased to see them thinking about appropriate choices."

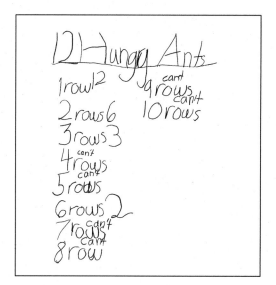

As children finished work, Marilyn had them find someone else who was also finished and explain their solutions to each other. In this way, children had opportunities to compare the results from different numbers.

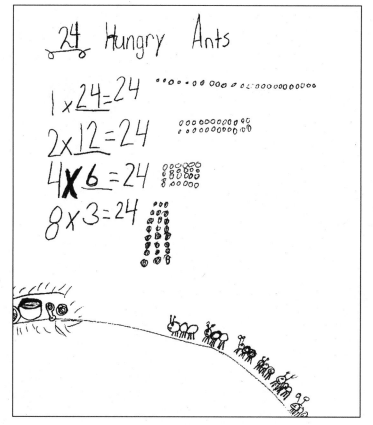

From a Third Grade Class

Dee Uyeda read the book to her third graders after they had been studying multiplication and division. She asked the children to choose a number to explore, but she didn't give any suggestions or set any limits. Also, she integrated a writing experience into the math assignment, asking the children to write stories similar to *One Hundred Hungry Ants*, but using their own numbers and any other characters or settings that they would like. Dee told the children that they could work individually or in pairs.

"There are two parts you have to do and one more you can choose to do if you like," Dee explained. The two required parts were for children to write the story and to explain how they figured out the mathematics. The optional part was to draw pictures to illustrate their stories.

The different characters the children chose included swarming bees, migrating birds, elephants, mice, snakes, and book worms. Several pairs chose 120, the smallest number chosen; the other numbers included 150, 160, 200, 400, and 800.

Erica and Jamie wrote about elephants and limousines, explained their math thinking, and included an illustration.

120 Elephants

120 Elephants were geting ready for a dance. They wanted to get there early so they could here the first song and the first song was the best. So they started to walk. They were almost there intill the middle size one said "Stop we should go home and rent one limmeo, and then we will get there faster."

So they went home and rented one limmeo. 120 elephants were in the limmeo then the yongest one said "I am squished!" So the elephants got two limmeos. So their two limmeos each had 60 elephants in it. Then the oldest said "I am squished!" So the elephats rented three limmeos. They put 40 elephants in each limmeo. Then the African elephant said "I am squished!" So they rented four limmeos. They put 30 elephants in each limmeo. Then the meanst elephant said "I am squished!!" So they rented five limmeos. and everybody was conterble. But when they got to the dance, the hole dance was over.

Marianne and Annie explained how they did the math for 400 mice.

Not all of the children found all of the possible ways to line up objects. For example, Joanne and Celia's story was titled "150 Hungry Book Worms." They wrote:

Off to the libray went 150 book worms. In a strat line. Down the street. "Stop" said the tallest book worm. "were going too slow the libray will close befor we get there. Split up into three lines of 50." It took them a long time. Off to the library. "Stop" said the tallest one. "Well neer get there in time. The libray is going to close. Split up into 6 lines of 25." It took them a long itme. Off to the libray. "Stop" said the tallest one. "There closed." 149 book worms chashed the tallest book worm all the way home. "It's not my failt you took too long to get in line."

One Monday Morning

Uri Shulevitz wrote and illustrated *One Monday Morning*. One Monday morning, a king, a queen, and a prince pay a visit to a little boy. The boy is not home, so the king, queen, and prince return with the knight on Tuesday. On Wednesday, the king, queen, prince, knight, and royal guard try to visit the boy. The group of visitors keeps returning and growing until the boy is finally home to greet them. The story leads nicely to creating a concrete graph and having children think about a counting problem.

I used the big book version to present the story to the first graders. As I read, children predicted the days. "Thursday's next," Kimberly said after we read what happened to the boy on Wednesday. Students also predicted who was coming to visit the next day.

I read the book with the class several times over the next few days. Then I asked the students to help me recall the story without looking at the book. Their response assured me they were familiar with the story, and I introduced the math activity.

"Today, we'll keep track of the number of visitors the boy had each day," I said.

I took out a bucket of Snap Cubes, and had the children choose a color to represent each of Monday's visitors. Nina suggested yellow for the king, because it looked like gold and he wore a crown. We chose red for the queen and blue for the little prince.

Harlan snapped one of each color together and stood the train of three cubes on the chalk tray. I wrote "Monday" above it, and then wrote the rest of the days of the week across the board, so we could put a train of cubes under each one.

Mary told the next part of the story. "They came back again on Tuesday," she said, "and the knight came too."

I asked, "What color cubes should we use for Tuesday?"

Chris said, "Yellow, red, and blue, because all of them came back, and one more."

"Who else can explain Chris's idea?" I asked. I called on Russell.

"We need the same colors because the king, the queen, and the little prince came back on Tuesday," he said. "But we need a new color for the knight."

Mary suggested green, and Russell made a new stack with yellow, red, blue, and green cubes and stood it up on the chalk tray under "Tuesday."

We continued this way until we had retold the story through Thursday, building a train of cubes for each day. I then stopped to check that the children were relating the cubes to the story. I picked up the stack under "Wednesday" and pointed to the orange cube.

"Who can tell me what this orange cube stands for?" I asked. I wanted to reinforce for the children that the cubes represented the characters in the story. I've noticed that sometimes my students lose touch with what manipulatives represent when I don't give them opportunities to keep making connections between the materials and the situations. Several hands went up right away. I waited a few moments to give more children a chance to think and then called on Ronnie.

"Orange means the royal guard," she said.

"How do you know?" I asked.

"Because it's at the top, and the royal guard came last that day," Ronnie responded.

Then I asked, "I wonder, how could we figure out how many visitors came on Sunday?" Everyone talked at once. "Count the pictures in the book." "Make more stacks of cubes." "We could act it out." A few children began counting on their fingers.

"I'm hearing some wonderful ideas," I said. "I'm going to give you each the chance to think about the problem, figure it out, and explain what you did." The children were eager to get started, but I quieted them and told them I wanted to talk a bit more so they would be sure to understand what they were to do.

"What do we have in our classroom that you could use to help you figure out the number of visitors that came on Sunday?" I asked. Students responded by suggesting just about everything we had on the shelves—cubes, beans, tiles, and links, etc.

"You can use anything you think will help," I told them, "but I want you to think about how you are going to use the materials before you take them off the shelves. Also, I'm going to give each of you a sheet of blank paper so that you can record your answer and tell how you solved the problem." To suggest how they might begin writing, I wrote on the board: *On Sunday __ visitors came.*

"You may use words, pictures, or numbers to help me understand how you solved the problem," I concluded.

The students began work in different ways. Some referred to the big book or to one of the small versions we had in the classroom. Some began writing right away. Others headed for the materials shelf. Some seemed at a loss for how to get started. I walked around, not intervening yet, but watching to see how each child approached the problem.

Mary drew pictures of seven people and a dog. When I asked her to tell me about her pictures, she identified each character in the story and then wrote letters above their heads so that I could tell who each was. "Every day another person came," she said.

"Can you write a number that will answer the question about how many visitors came Sunday?" I asked. I left her trying to think of another way to record her thinking.

Nina had more difficulty getting started. As I walked by, she wrinkled her forehead and said, "I don't know what to do." Nina often has trouble getting started on solving problems and looks to me for reassurance that she's on the right track.

"What do you think you might do first?" I asked.

"Copy the sentence off the board," she said, tentatively. She did this and then carefully wrote the numbers from 1 to 12. I told her I'd be back.

Russell used Snap Cubes to re-create what we had built on the chalk tray. He made stacks of cubes beginning with a stack of three and continuing in a stairstep up to a stack of nine. He was smiling and eager to tell me about his solution. After he explained what he did, I asked him to think about what he could write on his paper that would show how he had solved the problem. "I know what to do!" he said. He drew pictures of the stacks of cubes and wrote a number on each one.

Kimberly used the same strategy as Russell but explained that she also used the book to help her solve the problem.

Cal was finished before I got to his desk. He wrote: *i fegrit it at by 9.*

"How did you find that answer?" I asked.

"I looked at those cubes," he said, pointing to the stacks of cubes we had built and placed on the chalk tray. While it was easy for Chris to look at those cubes and think ahead several steps to figure out how many there would be on Sunday, it was very difficult for him to put his process into words. I wasn't too worried about his difficulty. I know that with many experiences of this kind, Chris would get better at explaining his thinking. With most things, practice is necessary for growth.

When I returned to Nina, I asked her how she had solved the problem. She smiled and said, "I figured it out with numbers."

"What do you think the answer is?" I asked.

She said, "I think it's a lot of numbers." I tried to interest her in trying to find just one number that would tell how many visitors came on Sunday, but Nina was perfectly happy with her answer. I agonize sometimes over how much to "teach" a child in a situation like this. I wasn't sure if Nina just didn't have a way to think about this problem or whether she really thought she had solved it and was happy with her answer. I left her singing the days of the week song.

The children's work varied. Like Mary, Sharon drew pictures to solve the problem and labeled each picture with an initial to identify it. However, she left out the dog.

Sharon drew the eight people in the story but forgot the dog.

Craig started to draw pictures of the cubes but erased them and instead drew pictures of the story characters. Maria drew pictures of cubes and characters and also copied the days of the week at the bottom, but she didn't seem able to come up with a final answer.

The children's responses gave me hints about how individual students thought about the problem and the problem-solving strategies that made sense to them.

Maria started her solution using Snap Cubes, then seemed to get lost before finding a solution.

Russell used Snap Cubes and successfully solved and illustrated the problem.

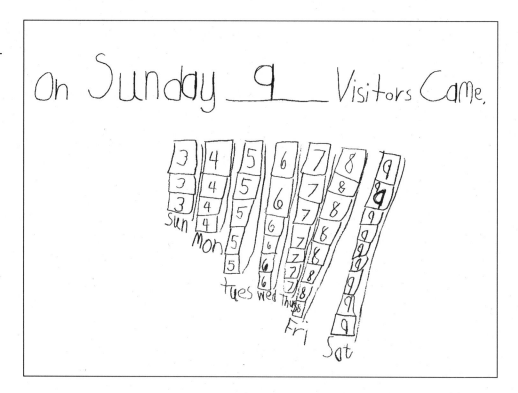

Only One

In *Only One*, Marc Harshman poetically assigns numbers to familiar things. He begins, "There may be a million stars, But there is only one sky. There may be 50,000 bees, But there is only one hive. There may be 500 seeds, But there is only one pumpkin." The next page skips down to 100, then to 12, and the following pages count down to 1, each time contrasting a group with a single object. This unique counting book gives students the opportunity to discuss things that come in groups of various sizes.

I gathered a class of second graders on the rug and showed the cover of the book.

"I have a book to share with you today that has some interesting mathematical ideas," I began. "But first, let me tell you about the unusual illustrations. They're called collagraphics." I read the description on the copyright page that explains how the collages in the book were made. The children listened with interest. Then I read the book to them.

"What did you notice about this book?" I asked after I'd finished reading it.

"There was only one sentence on each page," Kendra said.

"Every page has the same words, 'only one,'" Judy said.

"The numbers get smaller," said Jed.

"Yes," Wally agreed, "they started out really big and jumped down fast."

"Let's go back and look," I said. "The first page says, 'There may be a million stars, but there is only one sky.' The next number mentioned is 50,000."

Jed raised his hand. "If they went down by 1s, the next number would be 999,999. The book be too long."

"But it did start to go down by 1s," Karen said.

"Let's reread the book to find out where it starts counting down by 1s," I suggested. After 50,000 came 500, then 100, and then 12. From 12 on, the numbers decreased by 1s. When I read the page that said, "There may be 10 cents, But there is only one dime," Nikki was eager to comment.

"A dime is the same as 10 cents and 10 pennies is a dime," she said.

I turned back to the previous page and reread it: "There may be 11 cows, but there is only one herd." I then said, "I think the dime page has to be the page about 10, but the herd page doesn't have to be about 11. Why do I think this?"

Alex's hand shot up. He said, "A herd can be any number, but a dime is only 10 pennies." Others agreed.

Most of the pages in the book used words like "herd," "sky," and "merry-go-round," which might be used with several different numbers. But some pages had words that were number-specific, like "dime" and "trio." I wrote *Herd* and *Dime* on the chalkboard to title two columns and focused the children on each of the other pages in the book. As we talked about each page, I listed the topic in the correct column. The children were fascinated to look at the pages again and see which kind of page each one was.

Some pages created a good deal of discussion. For instance, the page that read, "There may be 9 players, But there is only one team" pictured a baseball team. Some students thought this made it a Dime page, but Scott pointed out that soccer teams have 11 players and basketball teams have 5. We finally agreed to put "team" in the Herd column.

Next, I asked the students if they would like to write a class *Only One* book. They responded enthusiastically. To get them started, I suggested they first think about things that might come in large groups. After a few moments, several children raised their hands. I called on Karen.

"There may be 10,000 people, but there is only one crowd," she said.

"Which column should that go in?" I asked.

"Herd!" the children answered in a chorus.

Judy raised her hand. "There may be a hundred dogs, but there is only one Clifford the big red dog."

Alex interrupted her. "That won't work. Clifford is just another dog. It's not like a herd or a dime." Alex had trouble expressing what bothered him, but he knew somehow that this idea was different.

I went back to the page with the herd of cows. "On this page a herd is made of 11 cows," I said. I turned the page. "Here, a dime is worth the same as 10 pennies. Judy, which of these pages is your idea like?"

"I'm not sure," she said. I told her to keep thinking and we'd get back to her.

Their ideas came as fast as I could write them down. For each suggestion, I asked whether the idea was like the herd or the dime. The children were interested and very involved in the discussion. Now and then there was a dispute, but they were able to talk it through. Some of the ideas in the Herd column were tanks (one army), jets (one airport), pencils (one pencil box). Some of the ideas in the Dime column were months (one year), letters (one alphabet), and states (one United States of America).

The list on the board proved helpful when we talked about how to organize the class book. We decided to start with large numbers, skip down to 12, and then count down from 12 to 1, the way the book did. The students had ideas for most of the numbers, but we were missing a few. For 11, for example, we had nothing listed on the board. Jed jumped up.

"I know, we can change the one about the tanks and the army!" he said.

"Never!" said Mark vehemently. It was his idea for the number 550, and he didn't want it changed. I pointed out that 11 tanks might not make a great army, and Jed turned his attention to finding a different idea.

Hassan pointed to the Herd column. "Those are the ones that could be another number," he said. We decided to use the jets and airport idea for 11, and moved on.

Each child claimed an idea to write and illustrate, and the book was on its way. Most children were interested in writing and illustrating the sentences they had contributed. Three students were so interested in the activity that they went on to write their own *Only One* books.

(Examples of student work appear on the next two pages.)

These pages from the
class book were Herd
examples.

There maybe 5 people,
but there is only one family.

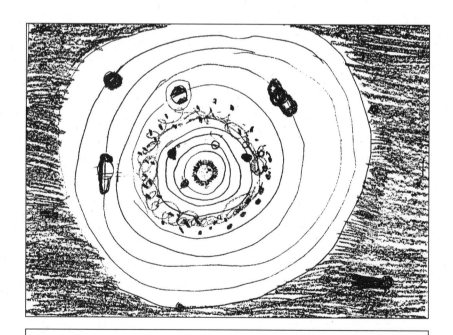

There may be 9 planets,
but there is only one
solar system.

These two pages belonged in the Dime category.

There may be 26 letters, but there is only one alphabet.

There may be five hundred fifty tanks, but there is only one army.

P. Bear's New Year's Party

"You are cordially invited to P. BEAR'S NEW YEAR'S PARTY! (Formal dress required.)" So begins the charmingly simple counting book, *P. Bear's New Year's Party,* by Paul Owen Lewis. P. Bear sends party invitations to his best-dressed friends. At one o'clock, the first guest arrives; at two o'clock, two more guests arrive. Every hour after that, the number of guests that arrives matches the hour on the clock. The last page of the book asks the question, "How many guests came to the party?" The problem solving suggested by the book provides the opportunity for children to use addition or, if they're able, multiplication.

I shared this book with second and third graders. In both classes, I read the book once, just for the children's enjoyment of it, and then again to introduce the math investigation.

In my second reading to the second graders, I stopped after reading three or four pages and asked the students what they noticed about the animals in the story. Jason raised his hand.

"All the animals are black and white," he said.

"What other animals do you think Mr. Lewis might have put in his book?" I asked.

"Skunks!" Brent exclaimed.

"Penguins," Larry suggested.

Beth added, "Black bears."

I asked the class to check these predictions as I read. The children were interested in finding out if their predictions were right. When I finished the story, Jamie raised her hand. "We were right about the penguins, but we forgot about pandas," she said.

Before I read the book a second time, I told the children to see what they could notice about the illustrations. "The author put some interesting details in the pictures that I want you to look for," I told them.

When I finished reading, I asked, "What did you notice?"

"All the pictures are black and white," Scott said, "except for the flag on the mailbox and P. Bear's bow tie. They're red."

"It's daytime at the beginning and night at the end," Audrey noticed.

"I know one," Jason said. "The time on the clock is in red and so is the word that says what time it is."

"The number of animals that comes matches the time!" Jane said.

"Wow, there's a lot to notice in this book," I said. "What do you think about the question at the end? Do you think you could figure out how many guests came to P. Bear's party?"

"Yes!" the class chorused.

I continued with the directions. "I want you to work in pairs and figure out the total number of guests that came to P. Bear's party," I said. "But I'm interested in more than just your answer. I'm also interested in your thinking about how you solved this problem. You may use anything in the room that will help you. On your paper I want you to tell exactly what you did to solve the problem. You can use numbers, words, pictures, or any combination of these."

The energy in the room was evident as they got started. The children felt confident about solving the problem. I find the more opportunities children have to solve problems, the more comfortable they become approaching them. The students in this class have learned that although they might need a few tries, they are capable of making sense of difficult problems.

Melanie and Jose headed for the bin of Snap Cubes. They made stacks of cubes, arranged them like stairsteps, and counted them.

Brent and Timothy made tally marks to represent the guests. They noticed a pattern in the tallies, that each of their subtotals was a "doubles plus one" fact. Although they thought this was a great discovery, they still needed to resort to counting the lines to find their answer.

Scott and Jason listed the numbers from 1 to 12 on their paper. They added the numbers in pairs—1 + 2, then 3 + 4, then 5 + 6, etc.—to get subtotals. Then they added the subtotals in pairs, and continued this way until they had only two numbers to add. I noticed Amelia and Larry pointing to the clock on the wall, and I asked them to tell me what they were thinking. Amelia said, "There's a clock in the book, so we're using the clock to add the numbers." When I walked by later, they had added tally marks to their paper. Larry looked up as I watched them work. "We wanted to be sure," he said.

Scott and Jason added the numbers from 1 to 12 by combining the addends two at a time.

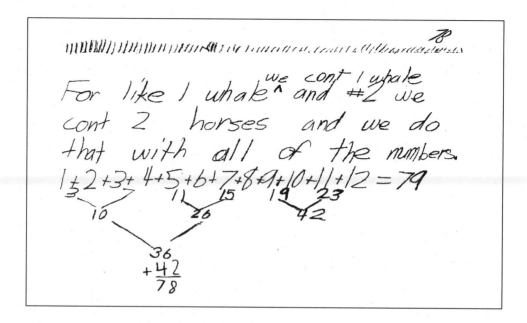

Emma and Jolie started drawing pictures, but they also switched to tally marks when drawing became tedious. As I watch children work, one thing I look for is their willingness to move from one strategy that isn't working to another.

Emma and Jolie started by drawing pictures and then switched to tally marks. Somewhere along the way, however, they miscounted.

Timothy and Brent raised their hands and called me over to look at their paper. They explained their solution to me, and were ready for a new challenge. I decided to suggest a follow-up problem and give it to the whole class. I asked the children for their attention and posed another question.

"P. Bear wanted to give out party favors at the end of his party," I said. "Since his party was ending late at night, he decided to give out slippers. How many pairs of slippers will P. Bear need to order?" Stuart's hand shot up.

"What about the killer whale?" he asked. "He doesn't have any feet, so he won't get a party favor." This idea seemed unacceptable, so Stuart suggested that the whale should get one pair of "flipper slippers." Everyone agreed.

Brent and Timothy got to work on this problem, and the others returned to working on the first question. I listened to Brent and Timothy talk about the slipper question.

"Some of the animals have four feet, but some have two," Timothy said.

"Yeah, like geese only need two slippers because they can't wear them on their wings, " Brent added.

The boys started to make tally marks for slippers as they retold the story together. However, they soon abandoned this strategy and went to get cubes. They stacked them to represent each page, starting with a stack of two cubes for the whale's flippers. Then they made a stack of eight with four each of two colors. I asked them about it. "Four red for one horse and four blue for the other one," Brent said. As I left, they continued to make stacks of cubes, but clearly the method was getting cumbersome for them.

Amelia and Larry also finished the first problem and were interested in the slipper question. As they went through the guest list, they used their fingers to count. They wrote down the name of each animal and the number of slippers it would need. Amelia was frowning as I walked by. I stopped and watched them work.

"I don't know if we're getting them all," Amelia said. "It's hard to keep up when you count on your fingers."

"But we can't think of another way to do it," Larry added.

"Why don't you look at how other groups are working and see if you get any ideas from them?" I suggested. When I returned a few minutes later, I saw Larry and Amelia still using their fingers, but making tallies on another sheet of paper to check.

When all the groups had finished solving the first problem of finding the number of guests at the party, I called the class together on the rug for sharing. I asked pairs of children to stand up, share their answers, and explain how they had solved the problem. Presentations like these are valuable because when children are so intent on their own solutions, they don't have the chance to consider other ways to solve the problem.

As the first pair shared, the other children listened and looked back at their papers to see if the answers matched. As children presented their solutions, it was hard at times for others to understand because they were so connected to their own strategies. However, I still think it's very important for children to get in the habit of listening to other ideas.

I asked questions to help the students compare their approaches. For example, after Brent and Timothy explained how they had solved the problem of the number of guests that P. Bear invited, I asked them how their solution was like Melanie and Jose's. "Our tallies are like pictures of their stacks of cubes," Brent explained.

"I noticed when I looked at your papers that some of you got 78 and some of you got 79 as a solution," I said. "Why do you think this happened? Can there be more than one right answer?"

Amelia thought for a moment and raised her hand. "There has to be just one answer. If we counted all the animals at the end of the book, we'd get it."

"Maybe some of us counted wrong," said Jason.

Although the children seemed to be in agreement that there should be just one answer, they weren't particularly interested in knowing whether it was 78 or 79. Each seemed satisfied that his or her answer was right.

"I'll leave the book up here on the chalk tray for anyone who is interested in thinking more about whether there were 78 or 79 guests," I said.

When all the groups had had a chance to talk about the first problem, I moved on to the slipper question. I asked the children who had finished solving the problem to tell the class what they had done.

"But don't give your solutions," I said. "I don't want to spoil the problem for the students who haven't had time to think about it yet."

As I listened to students' explanations, I realized that although the children were interested in the slipper problem, it was difficult for these second graders. The numbers were awfully large for children who didn't have multiplication to use as a tool. I left the problem as an option and suggested to the students that they think about it if they were interested.

A Lesson with Third Graders

When I read the same book to third graders, the students were just as delighted with the story as the second graders had been. For them, however, the first question of figuring the number of guests that came to the party was not really a problem. It was just an exercise in addition. They were more interested in figuring out how many pairs of slippers P. Bear needed to buy. The children were

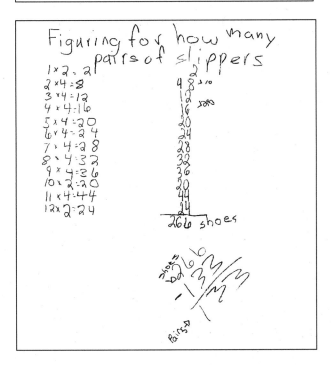

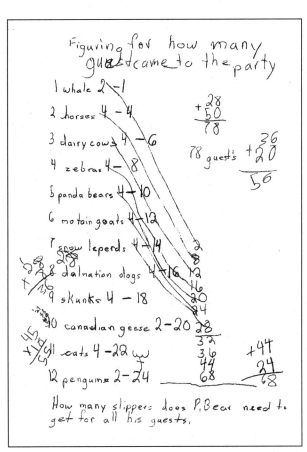

Annette and Loren explained their answers carefully and clearly and showed their work.

anxious to use their budding multiplication skills to find the number of slippers for each group of animals. They liked the fact that the numbers were large and the problem had several steps. When they shared solutions and how they got them, they were eager to show their own thinking and explain it.

Sometimes I don't know if a problem will work with a group of children until I try it. Sometimes the problem I suggest isn't of interest to them, or it's too easy. Other times, the problem is too complicated or the numbers are too large for them to deal with. Although my goal is to avoid frustrating children, I don't mind giving them a problem that causes them to struggle a bit. Even if they can't solve the problem, they always learn something in the attempt. My challenge as a teacher is to decide when to pull back, move on, or offer support. Watching children, talking to them, and listening to their ideas provide me with the information I need to make those instructional decisions.

Andrea and Katie added to figure out the number of animals and multiplied to determine how many slippers were needed.

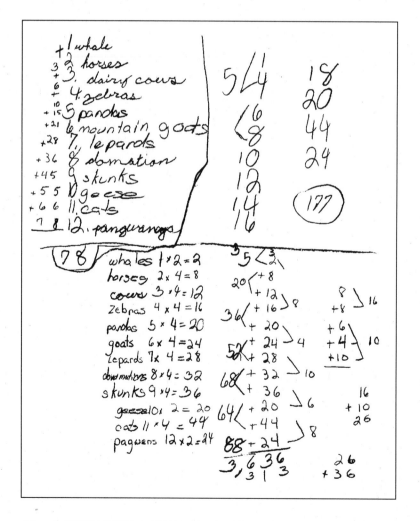

Peter's Pockets

Peter's Pockets, by Eve Rice, is a story about a boy named Peter, who puts on a new pair of pants and goes on a walk with his uncle. During the walk Peter learns that his pants have one serious flaw—no pockets! As Peter discovers treasures along the way, he puts them in his uncle's pockets for safekeeping. When they get home, Peter tells his mother about his problem. She sews enough pockets on Peter's pants for all of his treasures. The book suggests an activity that gives students experience with addition and place value.

As I read the book to first graders, the children kept track of the number of objects Peter found and put in his uncle's pockets. Later in the story, we counted the pockets that Peter's mother sewed onto his pants. I noticed some children were checking their own pockets as we counted, and this led right into my question for them.

"How many pockets do you think we are all wearing today?" I asked.

"I have two," Ronnie said.

"I've got a bunch because I'm wearing my jeans," Lamar said. Other children began to count their pockets and call out how many they had. After a moment, I called the children to attention.

"If we counted all the pockets you have, how many do you think there would be altogether?" I asked.

"Maybe 20," Reggie said.

"I think it would be 100!" said Timothy. As children guessed, I wrote their responses on the board. My recording their guesses helps the children see how to write the numbers they say. For some first graders, connecting written numerals to numbers they hear is valuable reinforcement. I continued until every child who wanted to had made a guess. The guesses ranged from 18 to 1,000.

"I have a special way for you to find the answer to our question," I then said. "I'm going to put a basket of Snap Cubes at each table. Put one cube in each of your pockets." I distributed the cubes, and in just a few minutes all the children had put one cube in each of their pockets. Sharon and Maggie were disappointed because they didn't have any pockets, but I told them they would have something special to do later.

"Now I want you to take the cubes out of your pockets and snap them together to make a train," I said. As the children made their trains, I removed the baskets of extra cubes from each table.

I noticed that Timothy had snapped his four cubes into a square. "Today, Timothy, it's important that you snap your cubes in a straight line," I said. He took them apart and snapped them into a train.

"Hold up your train of cubes so everyone can see it," I then said to the class. The children looked around at one another's trains and made comments. "Yours is the same as mine." "I have more; no, you have more." "Mine is longer."

I walked over to Russell, pointed to his train, and asked, "What does this train of four cubes tell me about Russell?"

Cindy answered, "It means he has four pockets on his clothes."

"And what about Colleen's train?" I asked, pointing to her train.

"Colleen has five pockets," Naomi responded.

"Everyone put down your train of cubes and listen carefully," I instructed. "Now hold up your train only if it has more than four cubes." I watched to see who quickly held up their trains and who had to count to decide.

"Okay, put them down again," I said. "This time, hold up your train of cubes if you have an even number of pockets." Several children held up their trains; others seemed unsure. I asked Nina how she knew her train of six cubes was an even number.

"Because I said 2, 4, 6," she answered.

Maggie held up her fist with no fingers showing. "What about you, Maggie?" I asked. "How many pockets do you have?"

"Zero," she said, "and that's an even number too."

I was impressed. "How do you know that?" I asked.

"Because 1 is odd, and zero comes before 1, and so it has to be even," she said. I was surprised by Maggie's response, and I decided to talk some more about even and odd.

"There's another way you can check your train to see if you have an even number of cubes," I began. "If you can break your train into two equal trains, you have an even number of cubes. Nina, try breaking your train in half and hold up the two pieces for us to see." Nina held up two trains with three cubes in each, showing that 6 is even. I asked that all the students use the same method to see if their numbers were even or odd. I don't expect all of those students to remember this mini-lesson on even numbers; I think of it instead as one of many opportunities necessary to help some children make sense of an important idea.

Next, I asked each group to put its cubes together and make trains of 10. "If you have extra cubes," I said, "leave them unsnapped." When the children were finished, I walked around the room and asked the groups to report the number of groups of 10 and extras they had. I stopped at Eddie's group first.

"We have one 10 and three extras," he said.

"How much is that?" I asked.

They answered in unison, "13." I continued walking around the room until each group had reported.

"Now that you've heard how many pockets each group has, how many pockets do you think you are wearing altogether?" I asked. I gave them time to think a bit and then called on Mary.

"I think 20," she said.

"Maybe 40," Colleen said. I wrote each guess on the board.

"To find out how many pockets we have," I said, "let's snap all of the extra cubes together into trains of 10. Then we'll count all of the 10s and extras." I watched as the sharing process began. It wasn't easy, as the children weren't too anxious to give up their loose cubes to other groups. Finally, they had completed all the sharing and trades. I called one group at a time to bring up its trains of 10, and had the class count aloud with me—10, 20, 30, and so on. I placed the 10s on the chalk tray as we counted. When we got to 60, only extra cubes were left, and we continued counting, "61, 62, 63, 64."

I asked, "How many groups of 10 do we have?"

"Six," they answered.

"And how many extras?"

"Four," they responded.

I held up one of the trains of 10. "Who can tell me what this stick of 10 represents?" I asked. "What does it stand for in our problem?" I think it's important to relate numbers to the contexts in which they're being used.

Lamar raised his hand. "That means 10 pockets that we're wearing," he said.

"So what does the 64 tell us about our class?" I asked.

"It means we have 64 pockets on," Eddie responded.

Before ending the lesson, I asked, "If we did this same thing tomorrow, how many pockets do you think we'd count?" Ronnie raised her hand.

"Maybe 15," she said.

Mark disagreed. "I think we'd have more than today. Maybe 70."

"Why do you think that Mark?" I asked.

"Because maybe everybody would wear clothes with more pockets tomorrow," he said. I recorded both of their predictions on chart paper. I asked for other predictions and recorded them as well.

"Let's see what happens. We'll count again tomorrow and see how many pockets we have," I said.

Each day, for the next four days, we counted our pockets in the same way and recorded the total. Often during the process I stopped and asked the children what the cubes represented. Before we counted every day, we estimated the number of pockets we had. As the week went on, although some of the children continued to make unreasonable guesses, many others were able to use the information we were gathering to help them make closer estimates. An activity such as this gives children the kind of experience that helps them develop number sense and a beginning understanding of the 10s and 1s structure of our number system.

Pigs Will Be Pigs

Pigs Will Be Pigs, by Amy Axelrod, is a brightly illustrated tale of the Pig family's search for enough money to feed the whole family. The Pigs begin tearing the house apart looking for loose change and forgotten bills. They put all the money they find in a shoe box and head for their favorite restaurant, the Enchanted Enchilada, where they eat until they are stuffed. The story provides a context for lessons that focus on the values of coins and bills and provide practice with adding money.

I read this book to third graders as they were beginning to work with decimals. It provided a wonderful way to talk about how decimals are used to represent money numerically. As soon as the hunt began in the story, we started keeping track of the total amount of money the Pigs found.

First, Mr. Pig finds his lucky two-dollar bill. Then Mrs. Pig searches in her bedroom and finds two nickels, five pennies, and one quarter.

"Let's see, how much do they have now?" I asked. "Two nickels is . . . ?"

"10 cents!" several children responded.

"And five pennies is five cents," said Tamara. "That's 15 cents," she said.

"Mrs. Pig also found a quarter. How much is that?" I asked.

"A quarter is 25 cents," said Marco, "but I don't know how much that is altogether."

"Let's write all the amounts on the board and add them together," I suggested. "Carey, why don't you go to the board and be our first recorder. We'll record each amount the Pig family finds. What did they find first?"

Carey said, "Mr. Pig found two dollars," and he wrote *$2.00* on the board.

"Next, Mrs. Pig found two nickels," I said. Carey wrote *$.50* under *$2.00.*

"No, that says 50 cents," Esperanza said. Carey erased the *$.50* and wrote $.10 Carey also wrote $.05 and $.25, neatly lining up the decimal points.

"When we add money, it helps to keep the columns lined up," I commented. "That way, you keep the coins separate from the dollars."

Carey wrote the four amounts in a column and drew a line underneath. Then, starting with the dollars, he added. He wrote a 2 in the dollars column and then a 3 in the dimes column. Then Carey stopped as he looked ahead to the pennies. Seeing that he had to add 5 and 5, he erased the 3 and wrote a 4 in the dimes column and a zero under the pennies.

$$
\begin{array}{r}
\$2.00 \\
\$\ .10 \\
\$\ .05 \\
\$\ .25 \\
\hline
\$2.40
\end{array}
$$

I asked Simone to be our next recorder. For this page we discussed how much six dimes was, and how much 200 pennies made. Simone said, "That's two dollars and 60 cents." She recorded $2.60 under the $2.40. We continued this way, keeping a running total until all the money was represented.

The children were delighted by the restaurant menu in the book. We spent some time talking about the choices and reading each menu item. The children, since they lived in Texas, were able to describe their favorite Southwest foods. They all agreed that the special sounded delicious.

Our next task was to figure out how much the family spent on the specials. "That's a hard problem!" Gayle exclaimed. She came up to the board and wrote: $7.99 + 7.99 + 7.99 + 7.99 =

"It would be easier if it was $8.00," Esperanza said. "That would be like 8 times 4," she said, and she thought for a minute. "That's 32."

"Would our answer be more or less than 32?" I asked.

"Less, because the specials only cost $7.99 each," Nolan said.

"Talk to the person next to you about what the price would be for four specials," I said.

After a few minutes I called on Janine. "We think it's $31.96."

"Can you explain how you figured that out?" I asked.

Janine said, "Each special is a penny less than $8.00, so that's 4 pennies less than 32 dollars."

"Did anyone figure it a different way?" I asked. Neil raised his hand. "We started at $32.00 and we counted backwards four."

The last page of the book has a question at the top: "How much money did the Pigs find on their hunt?" It goes on to tell how much each member of the Pig family found and pictures the coins and bills. We checked our total ($33.67) with the total in the book and found we were one dollar off. Going back and checking our addition on the board, we didn't find any mistakes. We opened the book and started to go through the pages again. We solved the mystery when we discovered the page showing Mr. Pig with the one dollar he had in his wallet at the start.

Next, I asked, "How much money did the Pigs have left from their $34.67 after they paid $31.96 for their dinners?" I had students work in pairs to figure out the answer and then share their solutions with the whole class. Some students used the standard subtraction algorithm, and others counted on from $31.96 to $34.67.

Another Lesson with Third Graders

After Rusty Bresser read this book to his third graders, he had the students estimate how much money the Pigs collected. Rusty recorded all of the students' guesses on the board and was surprised at how close some of them were. Greg guessed $34.50, Timothy guessed $34.00, and Janine guessed $30.05.

Rusty read the book a second time and suggested that the students take notes this time so they could figure out later how much money the Pigs had. The children went to their desks, got pencils

Makito wrote and illustrated each amount of money that occurred in the story.

and paper, and returned to the front of the room. When he finished reading, Rusty directed the students to figure out how much money the Pig family had collected.

Amelia immediately went to get a calculator. "Amelia always tries to use a calculator first," Rusty reported. "Sometimes this is helpful for her, and sometimes it gets her in trouble. This time she got into a mess because she wasn't sure how to use the key with the decimal point. Timothy tried to help her, but she wanted to do it herself. Eventually, Amelia wrote down all the dollar amounts on the left side of her paper and the cents on the right. She added them separately, coming up with $32.00 and $2.27. Then she added these to get a total of $34.27."

Amelia wrote all the dollars on the left side of her paper and all the cents on the right, then added the two totals together to get $34.27.

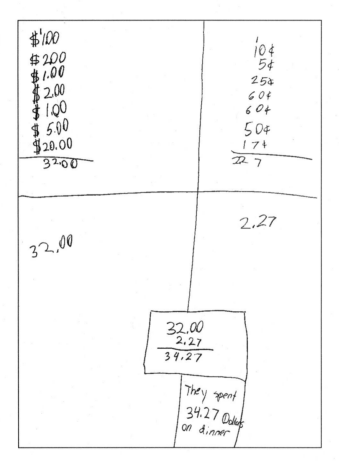

Sam lined up all the dollar amounts in a column and added them; then he did the same with the cents. He took the two totals and added them. To prove to himself that he had the right answer, Sam painstakingly drew pictures of all the coins and bills and labeled

them carefully. He was totally focused on his work and pleased with his results. His answer was $34.84.

George kept track in a different way. He wrote down the names of the coins and bills and, as Rusty read, George made tally marks next to the coins as he heard them read. However, he was not able to use this information to find a total.

Janine divided her paper into four parts. In the top two sections she kept track of what Mr. and Mrs. Pig found, and next to that she recorded the amounts and added them. In the bottom two sections she put the money the piglets found and wrote the values of the bills and coins alongside. To add the numbers, she clumped a few amounts together at a time and came up with partial totals. Then she added these together to get her final total. In the end, Janine was only 10 cents off.

Amber recorded the amounts first and went back and added the numbers on the side, keeping a running total. Although she had written $34.00 to start with, she later erased that and recorded her answer as $40.00. She wrote: *I added it by putting them together. I think thats the aswer.*

After everyone had a chance to work on the problem, Rusty called the class back together. He asked students to share how they had solved the problem, and he recorded all the different amounts they came up with. Then, together, they added the amounts from the book to find the total of $34.67.

For a follow-up lesson, Rusty wrote a shortened version of the menu on chart paper. He wrote the names of the food items (without their descriptions), with the prices alongside. At the children's request, he read the book again. Then he asked the students to look at the menu on the chart paper and decide what the Pig family might have ordered instead of the specials. He suggested that if students wanted to read the complete descriptions of the menu items they could look in the book.

"You need to remember that the Pig family had $34.67 to spend; be sure they don't order more food than they could pay for," Rusty said. "You'll need to write up their order as if you were the waiter or waitress at the Enchanted Enchilada." Rusty talked with the class about what an order form might look like.

"You also need to find out how much change the Pigs would have left over after they paid for their dinner," he added. Rusty reminded the children about using decimals to separate the dollars from the cents. He did this with a light touch, knowing that not all of his students were ready to use this information.

Rusty had students work in pairs because he felt it would strengthen their work and give them the support they needed to do the computations. He asked them, however, to record their work individually. As Rusty watched them work, he noticed how animated their discussions were. The children pored over the menu, talking about which foods they liked and which they hadn't ever eaten.

Rusty commented later, "They really enjoyed this activity. They liked being able to make choices. This problem is more accessible for students with different degrees of mathematical power. There isn't just one right answer, and allowing them to make choices made them feel they had control over the problem, which helped motivate them to do the math. In a way, they were creating their own mathematical problem."

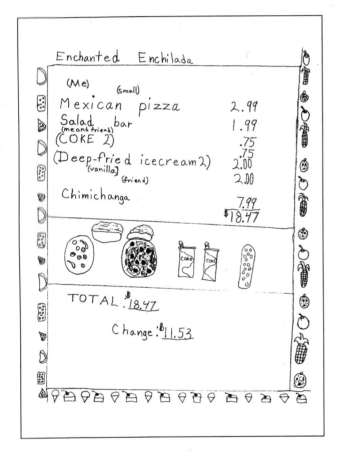

Sam designed a menu, selected foods for dinner, and listed the total amount spent and the change the Pigs would receive.

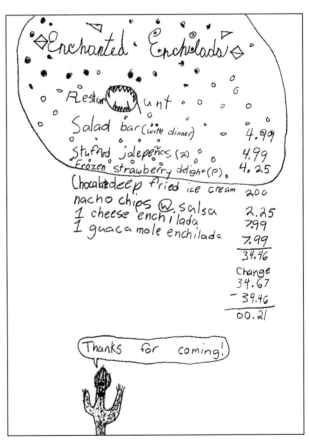

Tyler spent almost the entire $34.67.

Six Dinner Sid

Six Dinner Sid is a charming story by Inga Moore about Sid, an enterprising young cat who lives on Aristotle Street. Sid has convinced six people on the street that each is his owner and therefore goes to six different houses and gets six different dinners every night. First and third graders find different ways to approach the problem of determining how many dinners Sid eats in one week.

I gathered my first grade class on the rug. Before I showed the students the cover of this book, I told them that I thought they would be excited to see the main character. I pointed to the chalkboard that held the graph we had made the day before, showing their favorite animals.

"Cats!" Nina shouted. I displayed the cover of the book so that the students could see that Sid was indeed a cat.

This was the beginning of the year, and I was encouraged when Eddie read the word "Six" in the title. I read the entire title, and Kimberly immediately noticed and counted the stack of six bowls in the picture. I had the children predict from the cover what the story would be about, and then I read it to them.

The children enjoyed the story. As I read, Cal pointed out the pages that had six pictures divided in different ways. "3 and 3 makes 6," he said when he saw the picture of Sid eating out of six different bowls. When I finished the book, we talked about the differences between the two neighborhoods. I asked whether Sid really needed six dinners every night.

"We only feed our cat once a day," said Nina.

"I think he's going to get fat," Harlan added.

Next, I posed a question. I asked, "How many dinners do you think Sid ate in a whole week?"

"Six," Amy answered right away.

"No," said Timothy, "he had six just in one day."

"Oh, yeah," Amy agreed.

"How many days are there in a week?" I asked. We had been

working with the calendar each day, and the children answered "seven" in unison. I told them that they would need to use this information to answer my question about the numbers of dinners Sid ate in a week.

"Who can tell the question I asked?" I said. I usually ask several students to restate a problem. Restating a problem seems to help children understand and remember it. Also, having several children restate the problem gives students the opportunity to hear the question several times and in different ways.

I told the students what I expected from them. "I'm going to give each of you a sheet of blank paper," I said. "I'd like you to try to find the answer to the question, then write words or numbers or draw pictures to help me understand how you got your answer. You may use any materials in our room that you think will help you. When I read your papers later, I want to be able to tell what you used and what you did. You can work alone or with a partner."

I then asked students to suggest some of the materials they thought might be helpful to them. Mary suggested Snap Cubes, and other children mentioned beans, links, and tiles. "Any of these might be helpful," I said, "but you should think about how you will use the materials before taking them off the shelves."

Before I had the students return to their seats and begin work, I asked if anyone had questions. Sharon raised her hand.

"How do you spell dinner?" she asked.

"I'll write it on the board," I said. On the board I wrote: *Sid had ___ dinners in a week.* "You may copy this and use it on your paper if you want."

I distributed paper, and the children began to work. As I walked around, it was easy to tell who had an idea and who was still struggling with the question. I stopped at Eddie's desk. He was busily making trains with six Snap Cubes in each.

"Why are you making trains of six?" I asked.

"Because Sid had six dinners every day," he responded.

"Which day does this represent?" I asked, pointing to one of the groups.

"What does represent mean?" Eddie asked.

"It means 'stands for,'" I said. "Which day does this group of cubes stand for?"

"Sunday," he told me. As I pointed to groups of cubes, Eddie named the days of the week. He was surprised when he reached the last group and said, "Friday." He thought he had enough for the entire week.

"Did I already count that one?" he asked, pointing to one of the trains.

"I think so, but why don't you count again to be sure?" I answered. Eddie repeated the days of the week as he pointed to each train. Then he reached for the bag of cubes.

"I need another one for Saturday," he told me.

I left Eddie and looked around the room to see how others were doing. I noticed that Craig was also making trains with six Snap Cubes. Russell was making a long chain of links, using six of one color and then six of another. Ronnie had Pattern Blocks on her desk and was happily fitting them together to make designs. She seemed not to be considering the problem at all. I decided to give her a few minutes and check on her later.

Kimberly raised her hand to call me over to her desk. She had arranged popcorn kernels into groups of six and was excited to show them to me. I asked her why she did this, and she just smiled and shrugged her shoulders.

I find that early in the year, first graders often have good ideas and good problem-solving abilities but are limited in their ability to verbalize their thinking. That's why I think it is so important to ask them to explain their thinking. It pushes them to describe the mental processes they are using.

Kimberly found it difficult to describe what she had done. When I questioned her, she was quickly willing to abandon her idea, as if it must be wrong if I was asking about it. I assured her that she had great ideas but I wanted to hear her talk about them. Even as early as first grade, children sometimes get the message that teachers ask them to explain their thinking only when they have wrong answers.

I used a series of questions to probe Kimberly's thinking. "What's the question I asked you to think about?" "Why did you make piles of six popcorn kernels?" "How many piles did you make?" "Why?" My questions helped Kimberly explain what she had done. Her answers revealed to me that she understood the problem and her solution. I asked her to record her answer on paper.

"Can I draw pictures of the popcorn?" she asked.

"That would be fine," I told her. I noticed later that Kimberly had turned her desk to face the calendar and was copying abbreviations for the days of the week to label her picture.

Nina, Sharon, and Audrey were sitting together with cubes scattered on their desks. They seemed to be working together, but they were having difficulty deciding what to do with the cubes. I approached and asked what they were doing. They seemed con-

Kimberly made groups of popcorn kernels to find the answer.

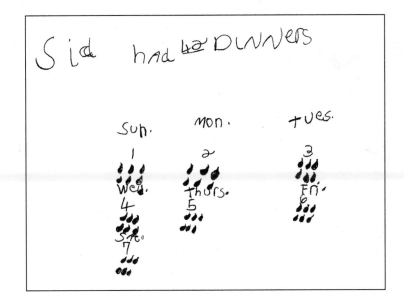

Sid had 42 Dinners

Sun.
1

Mon.
2

Tues.
3

Wed.
4

Thurs.
5

Fri.
6

Sat.
7

fused, so I asked them to restate the problem, a task that was difficult for them. In the minutes since leaving the rug, they had lost their focus on the problem and were now exploring the cubes, making patterns and trains the way we had for several weeks. I talked about the story and asked the question again, "How many dinners did Sid eat in a week?"

None of these girls seemed able to begin thinking about this question. We talked about the days of the week and the number of dinners Sid ate each day, but still the girls were confused and frustrated. I decided to let them return to their pattern building and made a note to myself about this discussion. Since my purpose in this activity was to give students a problem and assess their problem-solving strategies, I didn't feel it was necessary to push them to the point of frustration.

I continued walking around the room, making notes to myself about how students were working. I noted who chose to work with a partner and who worked alone. I watched to see which children used manipulatives effectively on their desks but couldn't translate their thinking to paper. This is very common at the beginning of the year, and often those students need encouragement to draw pictures of what they've done.

I went back to watch what Ronnie was doing with the Pattern Blocks. To my surprise, she was lining up rows of six of each shape and tracing around them. She had also drawn a picture of a cat at the bottom of the page. I was reminded that children often just need time to work out their own solutions. Ronnie is a quiet child who sometimes has trouble expressing herself and becomes frustrated. I was glad I hadn't intervened earlier.

Although this was a fairly difficult problem for first graders early in the school year, I learned a good deal about my students by observing them grapple with it. I learned that some of them need more time exploring the materials, while others are already comfortable using materials to solve a problem. I discovered that some children prefer to work alone, yet continually check in with others for reassurance that they're on the right track. I learned about the frustration levels of a few and the confidence of others. I didn't worry too much about children's answers, but I noted which children seemed concerned about getting the right answer and which didn't.

I think this problem allowed my class to think about numbers in a new way, to use manipulatives to represent large numbers, and to practice recording their ideas on paper. And for me it was a useful assessment tool.

Russell made a group of six for each day of the week. However, he miscounted, and his answer was off by 1.

A Lesson with Third Graders

When Rusty Bresser read *Six Dinner Sid* to his third graders, they were in the middle of a unit on multiplication. He asked them how many dinners Sid ate in one week when he lived on Aristotle Street. Rusty was interested in watching how his students solved this problem and assessing whether they understood the concept of multiplication and were comfortable using it.

Although Rusty had read the book aloud before, his students were excited to hear the story again. When he gave the class the problem, he didn't explain that this was a multiplication problem or suggest that they use multiplication to solve the problem. Rusty had the students work with partners, but each student had to record his or her own work.

Seth carefully drew the menu for each dinner to illustrate his answer.

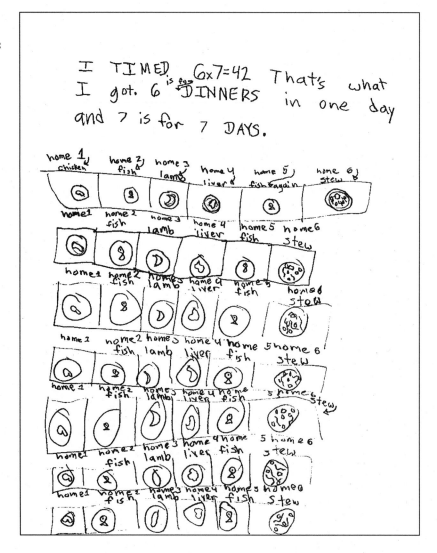

Scott solved the problem by adding 7 six times. He also drew a picture of six houses and wrote the number 7 in each. Although Scott used the right numbers, he did not explain his thinking. His calculations, $7 \times 6 = 42$ and $7 + 7 + 7 + 7 + 7 + 7 = 42$, tell more about the sense he made of this problem.

Scott added 7 six times and drew the houses Sid visited each day.

Dylan and his partner drew several pictures and diagrams showing seven groups of six and six groups of seven. Rusty commented, "This let me know they understood the commutative nature of multiplication." Although they had five diagrams with models of the problem, Dylan wrote: *The ansoir is 42 We did 7 × 6 and it = 42 We did it on a cocelate.* Rusty asked him why they had used a calculator. *We yousd a cacelate becaus I cod noln't figr it out and it was to had.*

Dana drew tally marks to explain her answer. She made seven tally marks and circled them. She did this seven times and also wrote the number sentence $7 \times 6 = 42$. Rusty said, "She just knew that 7 times 6 equals 42, and she tried to match her picture to the fact."

Amber correctly represented the problem with a multiplication sentence. Her drawing showed another way to represent a multiplication situation.

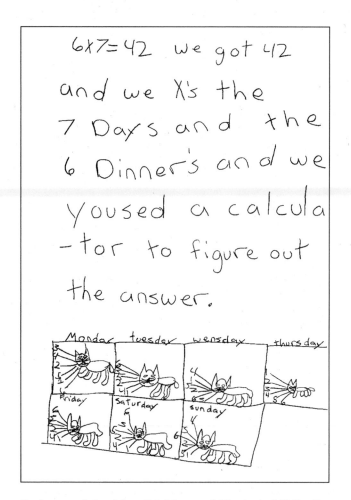

6x7=42 we got 42
and we X's the
7 Days and the
6 Dinner's and we
Youseed a calcula
-tor to figure out
the answer.

Monday tuesday wensday thursday
Friday Saturday sunday

Amber explained her thinking and illustrated Sid's dinners for each day of the week.

Jeremy first started to draw pictures to solve the problem. When this didn't seem to work for him, he moved to counting as a strategy. He was not comfortable counting by 6s, but he knew he could count by 5s. He told Rusty, "I couldn't count by 6s so I counted by 5s seven times, then added 7 to that to make 42."

"Jeremy always tries to let me know how he's making sense of what he's doing," Rusty said.

10 for Dinner

It's Margo's birthday, and she has invited 10 friends over for a party. In Jo Ellen Bogart's *10 for Dinner,* Margo's party creates many opportunities for students to think about combinations of numbers that add to 10. For example, three children wear shorts, one wears a dress, two wear jeans, three wear jogging suits, and one mischievous guest wears a Halloween costume. They bring birthday gifts, eat party food, and sing songs. Each situation presents a group of numbers that add to 10, providing children with an enjoyable experience with addition.

I read the book to my class of first graders, and the children were delighted by the story. They laughed when they saw that the earliest guest arrived in his Halloween costume and continued to be "different" throughout the book. Before I read the story again, I said, "This time, let's pay attention to the number combinations."

"Can I write them on the board like Drew did for the other book?" Kamila asked. Kamila was referring to recording the combinations the way Drew did when we read *12 Ways to Get to 11.* (See page 116.) I agreed. Kamila correctly used plus and equal signs to record number sentences for the combinations.

I led the children in adding aloud for each page. For example, the page about how the guests dressed describes three guests in t-shirts and shorts, one in a pink dress, two wearing jeans and western shirts, three in jogging suits, and one in his Halloween costume. We said aloud, "3 and 1 is 4, and 2 more is 6, and 3 more makes 9, and 1 more is 10."

Davy noticed that the number sentences Kamila wrote always ended with "+1," because the mischievous guest always does something different from the others. We looked in the book and talked about how the words had a repeating pattern: "But 1 guest . . . "

I asked the students if they would like to write a class book like *10 for Dinner.* They thought this was a great idea. I suggested that we write about our classroom.

"What would people see us doing if they walked in right now and took a picture?" I asked. I recorded their responses on chart paper.

"They'd see you sitting in the rocking chair," Calie said.

Selena said, "They would see the children on the floor in front of you."

Ian said, "They would see some children sitting up and some lying down."

"Yes," I said, "but let's get more specific about the numbers of children doing each thing." Soon we had determined that 11 children were sitting up, 6 were lying down around the rocking chair, Davy was getting a tissue, and Jane was putting her pencil in her desk. I made a sketch to match the directions on the chart paper. I sketched a stick figure teacher sitting in a rocking chair, with 6 stick figure children lying around it, 11 little figures sitting near the chair, 1 across the room, and 1 at a desk. We counted and found there were 20 of us, including me.

"But if someone took pictures at different times today," I said, "the pictures would show us doing different things. Let's make a list on the board of things we usually do in the classroom." I recorded the children's responses. The list included: Circle Time, Lunch Time, Recess, Music, Reading, Math, and P.E.

"I'd like each of you to find a partner and talk about the time of day that you'd like to write about. Then raise your hands when you're ready to choose." I waited while the children moved into pairs and discussed the items on the board. As students raised their hands to choose times to write about, I wrote their names on the board next to the items on the list.

"When you write your page for the book, you may use numbers and words or numbers and pictures," I explained. "When you think you've finished, have at least one other pair of students check your work to make sure that you've included all 20 of us."

Some children started by talking about what the class might be doing at the chosen time and writing as they talked. Others started by drawing a picture, then wrote numbers and words to match it. All students had to count carefully to be sure they had exactly 20 people in their pictures and had described what everyone was doing.

This activity was a good way for students to practice their writing skills and create their own combinations for 20. After we put the book together and read it, we recorded their combinations on the board and reviewed them.

The children wrote about what class-mates did during circle time, lunch time, and math class.

At circle time, 3 kids were lying down, 11 kids were siting up. 2 kids were geting in trouble and 4 kids were being nice to each other.

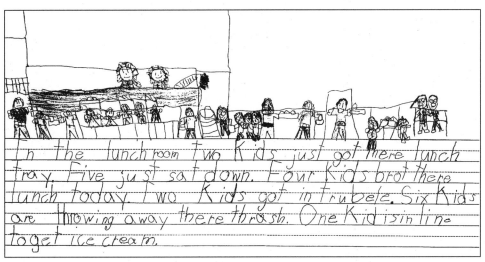

In the lunch room two kids just got there lunch tray. Five just sat down. Four kids brot there lunch today. Two kids got in trubele. Six kids are throwing away there thrash. One kid is in line to get ice cream.

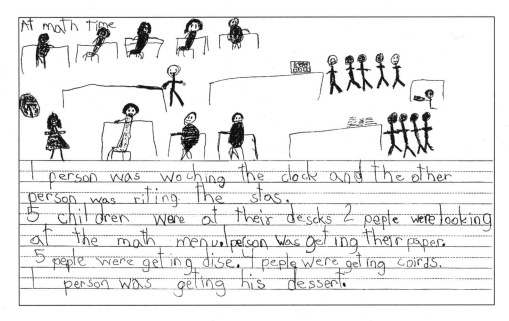

At math time

1 person was woching the clock and the other person was riting the stos.
5 children were at their descks 2 peple were looking at the math menu. 1 person was geting their paper.
5 peple were geting dise. 4 peple were geting coirds.
1 person was geting his dessert.

Ten Sly Piranhas

> *Ten Sly Piranhas*, by William Wise, is a counting book in reverse. It tells about 10 piranhas that disappear one at a time. Nine become the victims of a greedy fellow piranha, who in turn becomes a meal for a crocodile. This book, while a bit grim in its premise, is rollicking in its cadence. The bright illustrations invite children into the river world of sly and cunning piranhas. The story leads children into a discussion of subtraction and writing subtraction number sentences.

Before I read the book to my class of first graders, I asked if anyone knew what piranhas were. Since the children were not familiar with these fish and their voracious habits, I told them a bit about piranhas. Using our large class atlas, we located the Amazon River, where these fish live.

When I read the book, the children delighted in the rhythm of the words and the sneakiness of the greedy piranha. A few pages into the book, they began counting backwards to predict the number of piranhas left. They watched with glee as one piranha got bigger and bigger, and the number of piranhas decreased. "Look out!" they yelled, as they became aware of the pattern in the story and then chanted along, "And with a gulp and a gurgle—there were only eight." When I read the last sentence of the book, "And so ends the story of those foxy little fishes—unless you'd like to hear it told the same way again," the resounding response was, "Yes, read it again!" I was pleased to do so.

I then told the children I'd read the book a third time. "This time 10 children will act out the story as I read," I said. I chose 10 children and designated Kimberly to be the very hungry and crafty piranha who manages to eat all its fellow fish. As I read, Kimberly swam about, repeating the words the sly piranha used to trick its friends. After the first fish was eaten, I asked all the "fish" to stop moving for a minute.

"Let's talk about what just happened," I said. "How many piranhas were there to start with?"

"10!" they responded. I asked Conner to record. He went to the board and wrote *10*. "How many fish were eaten?" I then asked. After Conner recorded *1*, several children chorused, "And how many piranhas were left?" Others responded, and Conner wrote *9*.

"What kind of action took place on this page?" I asked.

"One piranha was eaten, " said Timothy.

"Yes," I said. "Let's write a sentence to tell with numbers what happened. Which number should come first?" The children responded with "10," and Conner wrote *10* on the board.

"What symbol do we use to show that something is being taken away from the group?" I asked.

"Minus," Sharon answered, "and we need an equal sign."

We continued in this way for the entire story, with the children telling Conner how to record numerically the action taking place in the story. This was not the first time we had constructed number sentences to describe a situation we acted out. Connecting mathematical representations to actions helps children learn the meanings of mathematical symbols.

After Conner had recorded several equations on the board, I asked the students to take out their small chalkboards. Then, as I read, each child recorded a number sentence to represent the action, while Conner continued writing on the board. As our classroom piranhas were eaten, they sat down and recorded on their chalkboards.

$$10 - 1 = 9$$
$$9 - 1 = 8$$
$$8 - 1 = 7$$
$$7 - 1 = 6$$
$$6 - 1 = 5$$
$$5 - 1 = 4$$
$$4 - 1 = 3$$
$$3 - 1 = 2$$
$$2 - 1 = 1$$
$$1 - 1 = 0$$

After we finished reading the book, I asked the students to look for patterns in the number sentences. Mary raised her hand.

"These numbers are going down by one," she said, pointing to the first column of numbers.

"And so are these," Anita added, pointing to the answers.

"Why doesn't this number change?" I asked, indicating the 1 in each equation.

Timothy answered, "That's the one piranha that gets eaten every time."

This lesson was valuable for the students. It gave children the opportunity to connect the symbols we use in mathematics to a situation of interest to them. However, learning how symbols connect to situations comes only from repeated experiences over time. Children need many such opportunities to internalize the meaning of symbols such as the minus and equals signs.

12 Ways to Get to 11
and
"Band-Aids"

In *12 Ways to Get to 11*, Eve Merriam combines different objects to make groups of 11. Nine pinecones from the forest floor and two acorns, one sow and 10 baby piglets, and three sets of triplets and a pair of twins are examples of combinations of items that add up to 11. Colorful, bold illustrations make this book especially appealing to children. The story presents the stimulus for students to discuss other combinations that total 11.

   Shel Silverstein's poem "Band-Aids," from *Where the Sidewalk Ends*, is about a child who gets a little overzealous with Band-Aids and ends up plastered with them. The poem also provides a springboard to creating number sentences.

I showed the cover of *12 Ways to Get to 11* to my first graders and asked them if they knew how to count to 11. The answer was a resounding "Yes!" and they all counted easily to 11.

Then I asked, "Do you know any other ways to count to 11?" They tried counting by 2s and 5s, but decided that they couldn't get to 11 either way.

I opened the book and showed them the title page, which has the words and the numerals for 11 and 12. The copyright page displays the numbers 1 to 12 across the top, with the number 11 on the bottom as if it has fallen out of sequence. We talked about why the illustrator may have drawn them that way.

"It looks like 11 is missing," Shannon noticed, but then she spotted it at the bottom. The next page shows the words for the numbers 1 through 12, but it has only a blank line where 11 should be.

"See," said Shannon, "I told you it was missing." The following page shows a black magician's hat and the words, "Where's eleven?"

I read the first page aloud: "Pick up nine pinecones from the forest floor and two acorns." Some of the children knew that 9 and 2 make 11, and some counted on their fingers, but all of them realized they had found the 11 on that page. The same was true for the next page, which showed six peanut shells and five pieces of popcorn.

But the third page was more of a challenge because three different things were put together to make 11: "four banners, five rabbits, a pitcher of water, and a bouquet of flowers."

Many students listened to the rest of the book without doing more figuring, although a few continued to try to keep up on their fingers as we read. I didn't make an effort during this first reading to focus on the combinations; I just wanted the children to enjoy the book.

When I got to the end of the book, I asked the children if they were sure there were really 11 things on each page. They seemed to accept that there were, simply because of the name of the book, but I pushed them anyway.

"How could we be sure that 11 objects are on each page?" I asked.

"Count them," several children said.

I asked Drew to go to the board and be the record keeper. As I read the book again, Drew wrote the numbers that appeared on each page. For the first page, he wrote: *9 2.*

"It looks to me as if something is missing," I said, "because when I read what's on the board, it says, '9 . . . 2.' To make 11, we have to say, '9 and 2.' What symbol means 'and' in math?"

"Plus," said Ramon. "You need to put a plus between the 9 and the 2." Drew wrote a plus sign, and we continued.

After I finished reading, I reviewed what Drew had recorded. To give the children practice with mental arithmetic, I had them add aloud to figure out the total for each combination. I led the practice, saying, for example, "4 plus 5 is 9, plus 1 is 10, plus 1 is 11." Many of the students kept up with me, and the children who couldn't at least had the opportunity to hear the sums as they looked at the numbers.

Michaela had a suggestion about the number combinations Drew had recorded: "We should add 'equals 11' to them," she said. I asked her to come up and do so.

Then I asked the students if they thought there might be more ways to make 11. "Talk with your neighbor," I said, "and see if you can come up with any other ways that aren't already on the board."

Some students suggested new combinations. "How about 2 plus 2 plus 2 plus 2 plus 2 plus 1?" suggested Jessica.

"We could put 1 plus 1 plus 1, and keep going until we get to 11," Jack said.

Kendra suggested, "3 plus 3 plus 3 plus 2."

However, when Shelly and Melanie reported 6 + 5, Jack noticed that they had merely rearranged the order of a combination already on the board. We decided that since the order was different, it could be counted as a new combination.

After all of the students had reported their combinations, I wondered aloud whether we had them all. Hassan said he thought there might be a few more. Many children, like Renee, were unsure. I copied the combinations onto a chart, posted it on the wall, and encouraged the children to find new combinations to add.

A Different Lesson in First Grade

Before Min Hong read *12 Ways to Get to 11* to her first grade class, she thought the children needed an introduction to the idea that a sum could be made by adding more than two numbers. She chose to use Shel Silverstein's poem "Band-Aids," which begins: "I have a Band-Aid on my finger, One on my knee, and one on my nose, . . ." The poem continues with different numbers of Band-Aids elsewhere on the body.

Min wrote the poem on a chart and used it during shared reading time. She had the class read it together as a choral reading. And, as first graders often do with their favorite literature, it wasn't long before the students had memorized it.

After using the poem for several days during language time, Min asked her class, "How do you think this poem relates to math?" At first the children didn't see the poem as mathematical at all because the numbers in the poem were not written as numerals. When they reread the poem, however, they realized that the numbers were written as words. They had many ideas about what Min had in mind for them to do with this poem.

Feta said, "We're going to add all the Band-Aids."

"We're going to practice using calculators," Ramona said.

"What do you mean?" Min asked.

"Well, there are so many numbers to add, we'll need a calculator," she replied.

After listening to all their ideas, Min prepared them for the next part of the problem. She assigned each pair of children two lines of the poem at random. The children had to read the lines and write a number sentence that described the words. They could also choose to illustrate their two lines. Some children used cubes or other counters to model the numbers in their lines before writing the number sentence.

Students recorded the math sentence and illustrated a few lines of Shel Silverstein's poem.

One on MY kneeand
One on MY hose

Three on MY elbow
and nine on MY toes

1+1+3+9=14

When all the groups were ready, Min asked the students to come together to share their papers. At one point, the children thought Min had made a mistake and given two groups the same lines of the poem because two pairs had the same sum for their number sentences. Min had the two groups with the same sum go to the board and write their number sentences. It was a surprise to some of the students to see the different numbers that made up the sum.

The next day, Min brought out *12 Ways to Get to 11*. She read the book aloud twice for the children to enjoy. Then she read the book again, taking time for the class to create a number sentence for each page. She recorded their sentences on a sheet of newsprint. Min reported that at first some of the students' totals were not 11. She didn't correct them right away, but waited until they realized that "a" meant one.

When Min read the fourth page of the book, Marika suddenly exclaimed, "Oh, they all equal 11!"

Min reported: "From this point on, when the students counted the objects in the picture to write a number sentence, they didn't always get the addends right but they always got the answer right." Min's classroom is culturally diverse, and for many of her students English is not the language spoken at home. In several instances, the meaning of words became clear to these students as she read. One such word was "pair." Students were pleased with themselves when they realized that pair meant two. "Many didn't know that before," Min said.

The following day, Min asked, "If we had to make our own book, what number would we choose as a sum?" The class suggested 20, 50, and 100. Melissa said, "Well, why don't we do 10, because we always go to the number 10 in math." The rest of the class nodded approval.

Min posed another question. "We'll do 'blank' ways to get to 10. If we all pair up, how many ways will that be?" She allowed the children to think for a few minutes, then she paired them up and counted the pairs. "Our book's title will be *13 Ways to Get to 10*," she concluded.

Min asked each pair of children to write one page, showing a group of things, and to be sure there were 10 in all. "You'll also do an illustration for your page," she told them.

As the children started working, Min noticed that some of them started with the picture and added words later. Others began with the words, and still others wrote a number sentence first. Min circulated, observing the children and talking with them to be sure they had words and pictures that matched.

When all the students had completed at least part of the assignment, Min called them together to share. All the pairs showed what they had done so far, and the rest of the students offered helpful tips to make their pages better.

Lucas asked, "How will people know what the number sentence is if we don't tell them?" The children decided to make each page a game. Each pair put the words and the pictures on the front of the page and glued a library pocket on the back. They wrote their number sentence on a small index card and put it in the library pocket.

Before Min put the pages together to make a book, she decided to share the children's work with other students in the school. She posted the pages on the wall in the hall. Other students came by and tried to figure out the number sentences, then checked themselves by looking inside the pocket. Her first graders were proud of their work, and enjoyed watching older children read their book and solve their puzzles.

Frank and Adam chose a Halloween theme.

We went to the supermarcit and bot 4 orenges 2 apples and 4 Greyps.

Damon and Emma wrote about super-market items.

$$4+2+4=10$$

Two of Everything

Two of Everything, by Lily Toy Hong, is a Chinese folk tale about an elderly couple who find magic right in their own backyard. Mr. Haktak discovers an ancient brass pot in his garden and decides to bring it to the house. He throws his coin purse into the pot for safekeeping. When Mrs. Haktak accidentally drops her hairpin in the pot and reaches in to get it, she pulls out two hairpins and two coin purses! Mr. and Mrs. Haktak realize their good fortune and get to work doubling their valuables. The book is a springboard to have first and second graders investigate doubling numbers.

After reading Two of Everything to my first grade class, I asked the students to explain what the pot did. This question was challenging because most of the children didn't have the vocabulary to answer precisely.

"Whatever went in came out again with another," Davy said.

Michaela said, "Yeah, it adds two each time."

But Jack and Branford quickly corrected her. "Five coins went in and 10 came out," Jack said.

Branford added, "They didn't go from 5 to 7, like if they added 2."

Finally Hassan spoke. He is a quiet boy who thinks deeply about things. "I think it's doubling," he suggested.

"Yeah, that's right!" others chimed in. Although we had talked about doubles in relation to adding, not all the students transferred the word to this new situation. I reminded myself that children need to make connections for themselves.

I suggested that we write down some things that happened in the book so we could look at them. On chart paper I drew a pot in the middle of a line and wrote 5 coins on the left side of the pot. I asked the class, "If five coins went into the pot, what would come out?" Several students answered, and I wrote 10 coins on the right side of the pot.

Next, I wrote 1 hairpin on the left and again asked what should go on the right side. We continued this way, listing everything that went into the pot and came out.

Then I asked the children to think of something else that could fall into the pot. They suggested a chair, a pencil, and then a pair of shoes. I recorded each item, and we talked about what would come out of the pot each time.

I used the "pair of shoes" suggestion for a follow-up problem. "How many pairs of shoes would have to fall in so that everyone in our class would have shoes to wear?" I asked. This interested the children! I gave them time to talk to their neighbors. As I watched, I saw several of them looking around the room and counting; some used their fingers.

After three or four minutes, I asked for the children's attention and asked them to explain their thinking. I was interested to hear how they thought about the question.

Michaela said, "I counted by 2s because everybody has two feet."

"How did you keep track as you were counting?" I asked.

"I pointed to people when I said the numbers, " she replied. "But I had to do it again, because I got mixed up and I didn't know if I counted Davy's feet already." Michelle reported that she had done the same thing.

Jack offered, "I counted by 2s too, but I used my fingers."

"Show us how you did that," I said.

Jack held up his fists and showed just one finger and said, "Two." Each time he counted, he held up another finger. "My partner helped when I ran out of fingers," he told us.

Although I expect students to listen to one another as they share, I sometimes find that with children this age I am the person most interested in what they have to say. It's difficult for first graders to articulate what they are thinking—and even more difficult for them to follow another student's line of reasoning.

I returned to talking about what else might fall into the pot. "What if half an apple fell in?" I asked. Children disagreed about whether two halves or a whole apple would emerge.

"It's the same thing!" Jane exclaimed in an exasperated tone.

We wrote down more ideas and decided as a class what should go in the second column. Dwight asked, "What if 15 marbles fell in?" and Christa suggested, "I think three hair bows fell in."

When Branford asked what would happen if a pizza with eight slices fell in, Jessica replied, "You'd get two pizzas, but you'd have 16 pieces!"

Then I reversed the question and asked, "What would have to fall into the pot in order for $5.00 to come out?" The children were puzzled at first but then began to talk to one another.

"I think it's one dollar and . . ." Kylie began, and she turned her eyes toward the ceiling as she thought. "No, it's got to be two dollars, because 2 and 2 is 4."

"Then take half the other dollar and you get 50 cents," added Hassan. Hassan was sure about what he said, but many children in the class didn't follow his thinking. As we discussed the question, I could tell which children had had experience with money at home.

"Let's try it out with real money," Michaela suggested. I dug into my wallet for bills and brought out our class jar of change. Michaela took charge. She took four bills and a dollar of change, divided it between Ramon and Shelly, and then counted it to prove her answer.

Over the next few days we added items to the chart whenever a student came up with a new idea. Some of the items we added were: a box of crayons (16 and 24), a dozen eggs, and $50.00. Each time something was added to one side of the list, children rushed to figure out what to write on the other side.

From a Second Grade Class

When Marilyn Burns used the book with second graders, she reported that the children loved the story. "After Mr. Haktak found out that his purse with 5 gold coins became two purses with 10 gold coins and Mrs. Haktak's hairpin became two hairpins, the children's imaginations just bubbled," reported Marilyn. "They were a bit horrified when Mrs. Haktak fell into the pot, but soon broke into giggles."

After reading the book, Marilyn asked the children to figure out the number of gold coins they could put into the pot so that they wound up with exactly 100 gold coins. A few students immediately figured that one possible answer was 50.

Marilyn then asked the children if they thought there were other solutions. "It may take more than one try," she explained to the children. "Each time coins come out, put them all back in so they double again." The children were sure that if they could put coins in several times, there must be other solutions. They spent about half an hour working on the problem.

Some students tested a lot of numbers. Marilyn was pleased to see Jeanette, a student who has difficulty with numbers, diligently work away. By the end of the period, Jeanette had found that 50 and 25 worked and that 10, 2, 3, 30, and 35 didn't work.

Two of Everything

```
  5 0        1 0         2      3        30
+ 5 0      + 1 0       + 2    + 3      +30
-------    -------     ---    ----     ----
  1 0 0      2 0        4       6        33
 yes !     + 2 0      + 4    + 6      +33
 yes !     -------    ---    ----     ----
             4 0        8      12        66
 yes !     + 4 0      + 8    +12      +66
 yes !     -------    ---    ----     ----
             8 0       16      24       132
 YES !     + 8 0      +16    +24       NO!
  No!      -------    ---    ----
            1 6 0      32    +24       +48
  2 5        no!      +32     48        96
+ 2 5                 ----   ----     +96
-------      35        64    +48      -----
   5 0      +35      1 64               192
 + 5 0     -------   128                NO!
  100        70      NO!      96
 yes !     + 7 0
            -----
   34       1 4 0
 + 3 4      NO!
 ------
   37
 + 3 7
 ------
   7 4
 + 7 4
```

Sixteen of the children found that 50 and 25 worked; five found that 50 worked and couldn't find another solution; two didn't understand the problem and spent their time writing math problems. (These two students worked together and spent a good deal of their time writing everything twice—their names, the date, the title, and each problem. At least they understood what "twice" meant.)

```
Two Of Every Thing
Two Of Every Thing
1. 50 x 2 = 100
1. 50 X 2 = 100

2 1 x 100 = 100
2 1 x 100 = 100   — Put 1 coin in 50 times = 100
3 5 x 20 = 100
3 5 x 20 = 100

4
4
```

Most of the children who found 50 and 25 felt there were other solutions that they just couldn't find. Annette wrote: *There are more but they are to hard.* Her response was typical.

Eldon included 100 as a solution. He wrote: *You take 100 and never put it in the pot.* Others liked his idea and added it to their papers.

Alex, who is fluent and confident with numbers, reported three solutions—100 (never put it in), 50, and 25. He wrote: *I think I have all the ways because you have to have 12½ to make 25 in two.*

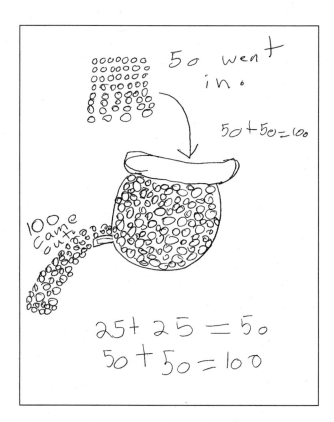

Two of
Eevery thing

$$\begin{array}{r} 64 \\ +64 \\ \hline 128 \end{array}$$

1. 100 never put it in
2. 50 100
3. 25, 50, 100
4.

I think I have all the ways because you have to have 12½ to make 25 in two.

Alex used his understanding of halves to determine that 25 was the smallest number possible.

0000000
0000000
0000000
0000000
... 50 went in.

50 + 50 = 100

100 came out.

$$25 + 25 = 50$$
$$50 + 50 = 100$$

Elena carefully illustrated her solution for putting in 50 coins, then used only numbers to show a second solution for starting with 25 coins.

Who Sank the Boat?

Pamela Allen's *Who Sank the Boat?* is about a cow, a donkey, a sheep, a pig, and a tiny mouse who decide to go for a row in the bay. The animals get into the boat one at a time, and each time the boat almost capsizes. Finally, the mouse causes the boat to sink. The story and delightful illustrations capture children's imaginations. Reading the story and using Cuisenaire rods to represent the animals help young children visualize combinations of 5.

Marilyn Burns read this book to a kindergarten class. She gathered the children into a circle on the rug and showed them the cover of the book. Several commented about boats they had been in. Some wanted to talk about toy boats they had. Marilyn told them that she was interested in their experiences with boats. "But right now," she said, "I'd like to read you the story about this boat."

Marilyn introduced the characters in the story, showing the class the picture of the cow, donkey, sheep, pig, and mouse walking on their hind legs toward the dock. Earlier in the class she had noticed Kyle, Alex, and Scott comparing the heights of two wooden figures and arguing about which figure would be taller if they weren't wearing hats. Marilyn told the class about the boys' discussion and then asked, "How do the sizes of the animals compare in this story?" After some discussion, the general opinion seemed to be that cows are really bigger than donkeys, even though the donkey was a little taller in the picture, that sheep and pigs are about the same size, and that the mouse is the smallest.

In order to provide the students with a concrete reference while she read the story, Marilyn decided to draw from the class box of jumbo Cuisenaire rods. She removed an orange rod from the box and held it up for the class. "Since you think that the cow is the largest animal," she said, "I'm going to use an orange rod to represent it. What color rod should I use for the donkey?"

The children were familiar with the rods, and several suggested the blue rod. Marilyn removed a blue rod and held it next to the orange one, so the children could compare their lengths. "Why?" she asked.

"Because it's pretty big and close to the orange," Conner answered.

When Marilyn asked what color rod they should use for the sheep, Katy suggested yellow. "It's littler, but not real little," she said. The class was willing to accept her choice.

"What about for the pig?" Marilyn then asked.

"It looks the same," said Mitch. "Use another yellow." Marilyn followed Mitch's suggestion. Then she asked about the mouse. About half the children answered, "A white rod."

Marilyn stood the rods in a row in front of her to represent the five animals and continued with the story: "They were good friends, and one warm sunny morning, for no particular reason, they decided to go for a row in the bay. Do you know who sank the boat?"

Some of the children called out guesses, and Marilyn reminded them about raising their hands. She called on several children to offer their predictions, and then called on Kyle.

"I know who sank the boat," he said. "I know the story."

To find out whether anyone else knew the story, Marilyn responded, "So Kyle and I already know for sure who sank the boat. Does anyone else know?" No one responded.

"Let's not tell," Marilyn said to Kyle. "Let's see if they can figure it out from the story." Kyle nodded his agreement.

Alex raised his hand. "Can we lie down and listen to the story?" he asked.

"Yeah, like this," Scott said, lying down in the circle. Several of the children, all boys, proceeded to lie down. This class had twice as many boys as girls, and they were an active bunch. Marilyn asked the boys to sit up and return to their places on the circle.

Before returning to the book, Marilyn asked the class, "How many animals are in the boat now?"

Several children answered simultaneously: "None." "It's empty." "Zero."

Marilyn reminded the children again about raising their hands and then asked, "How many are waiting on the dock to get into the boat?" Most of the children raised their hands. Marilyn called on Judy, who answered correctly.

Marilyn continued reading the rhyme that describes the cow getting into the boat: "Was it the cow who almost fell in, when she tilted the boat and made such a din?" The cow almost makes the boat capsize, but the next page reveals that all is safe.

Marilyn moved the orange rod to one side to indicate it was now in the boat and asked, "How many animals are now in the boat?" "How many are still waiting on the dock?" Some children knew the answers immediately, others needed to count the rods, and some just weren't interested in the question and waited for Marilyn to resume reading.

The story is cleverly presented so that a moment of panic accompanies each rhyme as an animal gets into the boat and almost sinks it. But when the page is turned, all is calm. Marilyn continued reading, moving the rods and talking with the children about how many animals were in the boat and how many were still on the dock.

At the end of the story, the tiny mouse leaps off the dock into the boat—and sinks it. The children were delighted.

"I have a question," Marilyn said. "How could a tiny mouse sink the boat after the four larger animals didn't?"

The class got quiet, as children thought about the question. Hands started to go up, but Marilyn waited so all the children would have a chance to think about the question. Finally, she called on Alex.

"It's because he jumped into the boat, and he wasn't careful," he said.

"Yeah," added J.P. "You're not supposed to jump when you get into a boat."

"That was my idea, too," Katy said.

"Does anyone have a different idea about why the mouse sank the boat?" Marilyn asked.

Maureen raised her hand. Always thoughtful, she replied, "It was just too much. It wasn't the mouse's fault. It was just too much for the boat."

Children's number sense develops over time from many experiences, and it's important to provide such experiences as often as possible. *Who Sank the Boat?* provides the chance for children to think about the combinations of 5 in the context of a story. Using the rods gives a way for children to visualize the combinations.

BIBLIOGRAPHY

Many of these books are available from:

Cuisenaire Company of America
P.O. Box 5026
White Plains, NY 10602-5026
(800) 237-3142

Allen, Pamela. *Who Sank the Boat?* Sandcastle Books, Putnam Publishing Group, 1989.

Axelrod, Amy. *Pigs Will Be Pigs.* Illustrated by Sharon McGinley-Nally. Simon & Schuster, 1994.

Bogart, Jo Ellen. *10 for Dinner.* Illustrated by Carlos Freire. Scholastic-TAB Publications Ltd., 1989.

Brisson, Pat. *Benny's Pennies.* Illustrated by Bob Barner. Bantam Doubleday Dell Publishing Group, Inc., 1993.

Burns, Marilyn. *The Greedy Triangle.* Illustrated by Gordon Silveria. Scholastic, Inc., 1994.

Burns, Marilyn. *Math By All Means: Place Value, Grades 1-2.* Math Solutions Publications, 1994.

Confer, Chris. *Math By All Means: Geometry, Grades 1-2.* Math Solutions Publications, 1994.

Fair, Sylvia. *The Bedspread.* Morrow Junior Books, 1982.

Felix, Monique. *The House.* American Education Publishing, 1993.

Friedman, Aileen. *A Cloak for the Dreamer.* Illustrated by Kim Howard. Scholastic, Inc., 1994.

Friedman, Aileen. *The King's Commissioners*. Illustrated by Susan Guevara. Scholastic, Inc., 1994.

Harshman, Marc. *Only One*. Illustrated by Barbara Garrison. Cobblehill Books, 1993.

Hong, Lily Toy. *Two of Everything*. Albert Whitman & Company, 1993.

Lewis, Paul Owen. *P. Bear's New Year's Party*. Beyond Words Publishing, Inc., 1989.

McCloskey, Kevin. *Mrs. Fitz's Flamingos*. Lothrop, Lee & Shepard Books, 1992.

Merriam, Eve. *12 Ways to Get to 11*. Illustrated by Bernie Karlin. Simon & Schuster Books for Young Readers, 1993.

Moore, Inga. *Six Dinner Sid*. Simon & Schuster Books for Young Readers, 1991.

Pinczes, Elinor J. *One Hundred Hungry Ants*. Illustrated by Bonnie MacKain. Houghton Mifflin Company, 1993.

Rectanus, Cheryl. *Math By All Means: Geometry, Grades 3-4*. Math Solutions Publications, 1994.

Rice, Eve. *Peter's Pockets*. Illustrated by Nancy Winslow Parker. Greenwillow Books, 1989.

Rocklin, Joanne. *Musical Chairs and Dancing Bears*. Illustrated by Laure de Matharel. Henry Holt and Company, 1993.

Silverstein, Shel. *Where the Sidewalk Ends*. HarperCollins, 1974.

Shulevitz, Uri. *One Monday Morning*. Aladdin Books, Macmillan Publishing Company, 1967.

Wise, William. *Ten Sly Piranhas*. Illustrated by Victoria Chess. Dial Books for Young Readers, 1993.

Wood, Audrey. *The Napping House*. Illustrated by Don Wood. Harcourt Brace & Company, 1984.

INDEX